The Ashtavakra Gita

Be content within yourself

English Translation

With commentaries by Christian Karl

The cover art shows a drawing of Sage Ashtavakra. The name Ashtavakra means eight ways. He was born with eight deformities on his arms and legs.

Table of Contents

Prologue to Sage Ashtavakra's Song

This spiritual scripture contains words of wisdom that can be contemplated over and over again, leading to a deeper and deeper understanding of the Self.

The Ashtavakra Gita, or the Ashtavakra Samhita as it is sometimes called, is an ancient Sanskrit text. Nothing seems to be known about the author, though tradition ascribes it to the Sage Ashtavakra - hence the name.

There is little doubt though that it is very old, probably dating back to the days of the classic Vedanta period. The Sanskrit style and the doctrine expressed would seem to warrant this assessment.

It is not really necessary to know a lot about the origin of this insightful scripture. Is it essential to know much about the origins refreshing trade winds of Hawaii? The importance is its enlivening and stimulating influence.

The work was known, appreciated and quoted by Ramakrishna and his disciple Vivekananda, as well as by Ramana Maharshi, while Radhakrishnan always refers to it with great respect. Apart from that, the work speaks for itself. It presents the traditional teachings of Advaita Vedanta with a clarity and power very rarely matched.

The Ashtavakra Gita is presented with numbered stanzas and my commentaries are indicated by the symbol >. I have thought long and hard about whether to keep the text in its original form where general persons are addressed as "he." That form worked well in the traditional setting of India, but it does no longer fit in with modern texts. Therefore, I decided to change the masculine form to the combined masculine/feminine form of today. Instead of "he" I will use "he/she," "him/herself," "his/her," etc. The text is a bit more awkward to read this way, but with time, one gets used to it. The only alternative would have been to have two separate texts, one in the masculine and the other in the feminine form.

Chapter 1 The Self

1. O Master, tell me how to find Detachment, wisdom, and freedom!

> This is the search all spiritual seekers are involved in. How can the Self be freed from the external influences so that it shines in its natural purity?

2. Child, if you wish to be free, shun the poison of the senses. Seek the nectar of truth, of love and forgiveness, simplicity and happiness.

> Involvement in the world of the senses leads to the attachment of awareness to material things. Seeking those values in life that are immaterial will lead to the natural detachment of awareness from material things.

3. Earth, fire and water, the wind and the sky [the five elements] - you are none of these. If you wish to be free, know you are the Self, the witness of all these, the heart of awareness.

> Your sense of identity lies within your own awareness. Your innermost sense of Self is found in and as awareness. The earth, fire and water, etc. are seen by this awareness. All is seen by this awareness.

4. Set your body aside. Sit in your own awareness. You will at once be happy, forever still, forever free.

> Awareness resides inside your body and is aware of all that is going on. This awareness sees the sense inputs, it sees your entire body, it sees your mind and your memories. Through the process of still meditation on the Self you will experience happiness and peace.

5. You have no caste. No duties bind you. Formless and free, beyond the reach of the senses, the witness of all things. So be happy!

> Awareness is your innermost nature. Awareness is the innermost nature of all living things. On the level of awareness only awareness exists, no differences such as castes, etc. On this level there is stillness. Here you experience the completion of all your endeavors.

6. Right or wrong, joy and sorrow, these are of the mind only. They are not yours. It is not really you who acts or enjoys. You are everywhere, forever free.

> Where there are no differences, there cannot be right or wrong; there cannot be high or low; there cannot be good or evil. If all is made from the same basic material, how can differences exist? If all shapes are made from the same gold, what difference is there between a bracelet and a ring?

7. Forever and truly free, the single witness of all things. But if you see yourself as separate, then you are bound.

> You are pure awareness, the witness of all. Whatever you see is seen in you. It is the Self that

observes all. An outside to you does not exist. All takes place inside of you, in your own awareness, your own Self. To see yourself as different from what you see creates the erroneous notion of the existence of "two or more." When you have this erroneous notion, then you live in constant search for happiness in "others," in an "outside." In reality all is going on "inside." All is going on in your own Self.

8. "I do this. I do that." The big black snake of selfishness has bitten you! "I do nothing." This is the nectar of faith, so drink and be happy!

> The notion of individual doership is the result of seeing yourself as separate from others. Because you believe in the existence of an exclusive ego, you have to maintain this ego with a number of actions. These actions are only necessary to maintain your separation from others, they are not necessary to maintain life itself. Your highest Self does not need your actions to exist. Self-awareness exists independently of your ego-maintaining actions.

9. Know you are one, pure awareness. With the fire of this conviction, burn down the forest of ignorance. Free yourself from sorrow and be happy.

> You are pure awareness that cannot be touched by anything other than itself. When awareness finds itself in its complete and innocent state, you are free from the plotting of the mind. When you find yourself in awareness, all anxiety and worries will simply melt away. You will find yourself in a natural state of being yourself.

10. Be happy! For you are joy, unbounded joy. You are awareness itself. Just as a coil of rope is mistaken for a snake, so you are mistaken for the world.

> In this natural state of pure awareness there are no restrictions as to how much joy you can experience. This state is filled with joy. You can stay in this state for as long as you please. It is quite exquisite. Your mental desires for this or that bring you out of it and make you seemingly lose the freedom you have experienced. However, the simple remembrance of the state of freedom will bring you right back to it again. This is the natural state to be in, not the state of confusion, worries and insecurity that comes with identifying with the body, mind and memories.

11. If you think you are free, you are free. If you think you are bound, you are bound. For the saying is true: You are what you think.

> There are many stories of prisoners who despite of physical restrictions, were as free as a bird inside their minds. Then there are some who in spite of all material freedom constantly worry about this or that and feel limited by their lives' circumstances.

12. The Self looks like the world. But this is just an illusion. The Self is everywhere. One. Still. Free. Perfect. The witness of all things, awareness without action, clinging or desire.

> When you look outside yourself, you project a sense of self onto your surroundings. Where does

that sense of self come from? It comes from within yourself. As the sayings go: "the world is as you see it" and "beauty lies in the eye of the beholder." The more beauty there is inside of you, the more beauty you will see in the world around you. The world is really only a reflection of your own mind. Be aware of life. See clearly that only you exist. See that what you are is pure awareness. You are the witness of your life.

13. Meditate on the Self. One without two, exalted awareness. Give up the illusion of the separate self. Give up the feeling, within or without, that you are this or that.

> There is only your inner awareness. This is your inner Self. Your inner Self is not your mind, and it is not your body. All is seen in this awareness. This awareness is one. You do not have more than one awareness. This awareness is you. You have a body, a mind, an ego, memory, intellect, feelings, etc., but these are not you. They appear in your awareness. You are aware of them. They can be taken from you, but awareness cannot be taken from itself.

14. My child, because you think you are the body, for a long time you have been bound. Know you are pure awareness. With this knowledge as your sword cut through your chains. And be happy!

> The notion that you are the body, or the mind, or your feelings, or your deeds, or your accomplishments, or your failures holds you prisoner in a cage. Your cage may be beautiful and diamond studded and you may find it very

comfortable, but it is nonetheless a cage from which you must set yourself free if you want to find the true happiness and peace of pure Self-awareness.

15. For you are already free, without action or flaw, luminous and bright. You are bound only by the habit of meditation.

> The realization that even this cage is only seen in your awareness and that it can in no way limit awareness itself will allow access to your natural state of freedom in the Self. The key to Self-realization lies in the conviction that nothing else exists but Self-awareness. All that exists and that can be seen is seen in awareness alone. The path to the Self is only blocked by one's own erroneous notion of imperfection. Where this notion came from, I don't know. All I know is that there is a way beyond it and that is through the acceptance of one's true nature as awareness.

16. Your nature is pure awareness. You are flowing in all things, and all things are flowing in you. But beware the narrowness of the mind!

> Whatever it is you experience, that is seen by awareness. Any stimulation of awareness produces feelings of bliss and joy. This stimulation originates in awareness and not in the things that lead to the experience. In other words, when you receive a gift that evokes feelings of happiness in you, it is not the gift that is the cause of these feelings, but the cause is the awareness which finds itself experiencing itself. This can easily be proven by giving you the same gift sometime later. If your pleasure really

resides in the object, then you should experience the same amount of pleasure both times.

17. You are always the same, unfathomable awareness, limitless and free, serene and unperturbed. Desire only your own awareness.

> Whether you are sitting or walking, reading or writing, you are the same awareness. Even if you don't experience it in this way, your innermost Self is pure awareness. In this awareness time and space do not exist. In it there is only existence, awareness and bliss.

18. Whatever takes form is false. Only the formless endures. When you understand the truth of this teaching, you will not be born again.

> To identify yourself with a particular form - this body of yours - makes you live in a world where birth and death are commonplace. Living like this your mind is constantly filled with fear of pain, suffering, and death. However, to identify yourself with pure and timeless awareness makes you live your life in peace and contentment, devoid of fear of mental and bodily harm.

19. For God is infinite, within the body and without, like a mirror, and the image in a mirror.

> The idea of God encompasses the highest, the purest, the Being beyond time and space.
The highest, the purest, the being beyond time and space that you can experience is your own inner awareness. I am not saying that you are The God, because many people have their own ideas and

concepts of The God; all I am saying is that all takes place in your awareness alone. That includes all thoughts and feelings, from the highest and most noble to the lowest and most despicable. In a sense, you are your own creation.

20. As the air is everywhere, flowing around a pot and filling it, so God is everywhere, filling all things and flowing through them forever.

> The highest you can experience is your own inner awareness. Nothing in your life can be outside of this awareness. Your awareness is carried by your body/mind structure. There are many body/mind structures in existence. All of them carry awareness within them. Your awareness is limited in its experience of the world by this body/mind system. But your awareness is not limited in its experience of itself. In awareness there is no space and time, there is only existence and bliss. Wherever there is awareness, there is the same unlimited experience of itself. Through meditation on the Self, you can realize this pure awareness at the core of your being.

Chapter 2 Awareness

1. Yesterday I lived bewildered, in illusion. But now I am awake, flawless and serene, beyond the world.

> The realization of pure Self-awareness happens in a moment. This is not a gradual process. It is instantaneous. You either feel the freedom or you don't. There is no in-between.

2. From my light the body and the world arise. So, all things are mine, or nothing is.

> You are the light of awareness in which all that exists is reflected. In this awareness your body and the whole world becomes visible. You can no longer say that something belongs to you while something else does not. All belongs to you now.

3. Now I have given up the body and the world, I have a special gift. I see the infinite Self.

> The renunciation of the world comes naturally when you find yourself as the pure witnessing awareness. The bliss and joy of this natural state overwhelm all desires for satisfaction in material things. Disinterest toward body, senses, mind, and the world is a normal outcome of the realization of the truth about one's Self.

4. As a wave, seething and foaming, is only water, so all creation, streaming out of the Self, is only the Self.

> All mental and material objects are seen by unlimited awareness. Look at the waves and foam riding on the surface of the unlimited ocean. What was there first, the ocean or the waves? The ocean. Therefore, the ocean is the cause of the waves. In the same way all of the various objects that can be seen by awareness are nothing other than awareness.

5. Consider a piece of cloth. It is only threads! So, all creation, when you look closely, is only the Self.

> Believing the sense objects to be different from the experience of awareness is erroneous. There is nothing that exists outside of awareness. All that exists only takes place within awareness and is therefore of the nature of awareness. This is similar to the canvas on which a film is shown. All takes place on the canvas alone.

6. Like the sugar in the juice of the sugarcane, I am the sweetness in everything I have made.

> The only true experience you have when experiencing anything is that of awareness. You become aware of something. What that something is, is not important. What is important is the experience of pure and blissful awareness.

7. When the Self is unknown the world arises, not when it is known. But you mistake the rope for the snake. When you see the rope, the snake vanishes.

> Seeing everything as of the nature of awareness, the notion of a material universe in which there exist differences vanishes. Both the rope and the snake appear in awareness.

8. My nature is light, nothing but light. When the world arises, I alone am shining.

> You are the light behind all experiences. You are the light in the projector that makes the film visible on the canvas of life. Without you as awareness nothing could exist for your body/mind system. Without you as awareness any sense of existence would disappear.

9. When the world arises in me, it is just an illusion: water shimmering in the sun, a vein of silver in mother-of-pearl, a serpent in a strand of rope.

> The world arises in you. Feelings arise in you. Thoughts arise in you. This world, these feelings and these thoughts are seen by you. But they are not you. You are the witnessing awareness. Do not identify with the world, the feelings or the thoughts. Only identify yourself with the pure witnessing awareness that you truly are.

10. From me the world streams out and in me it dissolves, as a bracelet melts into gold, a pot crumbles into clay, a wave subsides into water.

> When you look out into the world, you create a reflection of the world in your awareness. You cannot say that an "outside" world really exists. All

you know is what you are aware of. Therefore, the world arises and sets in you as awareness.

11. I adore myself. How wonderful I am! I can never die. The whole world may perish, from Brahma [the creator] to a blade of grass, but I am still here.

> You exist and you know that you exist. In this knowing of your existence there is the experience of bliss. This knowing of your existence is awareness. In this awareness there are joy and happiness. In this awareness there is the realization that you exist independent of external objects, people and things. You are self-fulfilled.

12. Indeed how wonderful! I adore myself. For I have taken form, but I am still one. Neither coming nor going, yet I am still everywhere.

> You love yourself as this awareness. In fact, you do not see "another" anywhere. So, all the love you have for life turns out to be a love for yourself. How wonderful! How ecstatic! How sublime! What bliss!

13. How wonderful, and how great my powers! For I am without form, yet till the end of time I uphold the universe.

> There is no notion of time in pure awareness. In pure awareness there is only the notion of being. You are this pure awareness. This is your true form, which is a formless form. As long as you perceive this universe as real, so long will the experience of the universe last.

14. Wonderful! For nothing is mine, yet it is all mine, whatever is thought or spoken.

> You have no tangible connection to the things of the world, such as body, senses and mind. Therefore, nothing can be said to be yours. But on the other hand, all appears only in you, so you can say that nothing is outside of you and therefore all belongs to you.

15. I am not the knower, nor the known, nor the knowing. These three are not real. They only seem to be when I am not known. For I am flawless.

> You are pure witnessing awareness with no specific attributes. You neither know nor do not know. You are neither here nor there. You are neither the knower nor the known. You simply are awareness. What you are aware of cannot restrict you, neither can it liberate you. You are always free and unrestricted awareness.

16. Two from one! This is the root of suffering. Only perceive that I am one without two, pure awareness, pure joy, and all the world is false. There is no other remedy!

> How can there be another to you? When you become aware of someone, this recognition takes place in yourself. Whatever you consider to be outside of you, that only takes place in your awareness alone. Find yourself in your own pure awareness and you will experience joy, bliss and deep inner contentment.

17. Through ignorance I once imagined I was bound. But I am pure awareness. I live beyond all distinctions, in unbroken meditation.

> The need to identify with body and mind is based on the erroneous idea that you are something other than pure and unlimited awareness. You are not a man or woman. You are not rich or poor. You are not healthy or sick. You are not ignorant or enlightened. You are pure and blissful awareness in which all takes place.

18. Indeed, I am neither bound nor free. An end to illusion! It is all groundless. For the whole of creation, though it rests in me, is without foundation.

> Even the notion of finding freedom in enlightenment is erroneous. You cannot find freedom because you are already free in your inner essence. You can only realize that you, indeed, are pure witnessing awareness living in freedom. The world cannot add to your freedom, nor can it subtract from it.

19. The body is nothing. The world is nothing. When you understand this fully, how can they be invented? For the Self is pure awareness, nothing less.

> Your body is an object of your observation, in the same way as all other objects of this world are objects of your observation. What is different about your body and the world? They both appear in your awareness. You are their witness. Why do you believe that one object is more important than

another? How can anything be more important to pure awareness than something else? All things are equally important. Nothing is higher, nothing is more important, nothing is more valuable.

20. The body is false, and so are its fears, heaven and hell, freedom and bondage. It is all invention. What can they matter to me? I am awareness itself.

> Identification with the body causes fears and insecurities. This body is undergoing constant change. Some of it is for the better; some of it is for the worse. Your need for security is based on a very shaky foundation when you look for it in your body. The same is true with your mind, your material possessions, and your friends and family. Find your own strength within yourself. Find it in the pure and changeless awareness that you fundamentally are.

21. I see only one. Many people, one wilderness. Then to what may I cling?

> Cling to no one. Only be aware of your need to cling. If you must cling to someone, then cling to a representation of God, whatever representation of God you feel attracted to. In order to overcome your tendency for selfish behavior, you need to love someone outside yourself. You cannot find yourself in an outside world, but you can learn to transcend your selfish behavior through love and compassion for another.

22. I am not the body. Nor is the body mine. I am not separate. I am awareness itself, bound only by my thirst for life.

> Awareness finds itself attracted to the various sense inputs it receives. It senses that there is something else in existence other than itself. Getting involved with these sense pleasures it forgets about its nature as pure awareness. However, what it finds when a desire is fulfilled, is the blissful awareness of itself. Awareness realizes that the highest it can experience is its own bliss. There is no other, nothing higher than itself. This realization makes awareness dispassionate about material things. It causes awareness to search out its own company. This process is called meditation.

23. I am the infinite ocean. When thoughts spring up, the wind freshens, and like waves a thousand worlds arise.

> Your imagination is infinite. That can be seen by the many movies produced every year that are based solely on imaginary events. Then there are thousands of writers who publish many novels based on imagination. There is no limit to the workings of the mind. All these outputs originate in pure awareness. Awareness is the creative originator of all that flows from people's minds.

24. But when the wind falls, the trader sinks with his/her ship. On the boundless ocean of my being, he/she founders, and all the worlds with him/her.

> When the mind comes to a standstill, all thoughts come to a halt. When that happens, only pure awareness exists. All thoughts are caused by creative impulses coming from awareness and fade away in the limitless space of pure awareness.

25. But O how wonderful! I am the unbounded deep in whom all living things naturally arise, rush against each other playfully, and then subside.

> On the surface of your awareness all of creation interacts playfully. Is there any purpose to this interaction? Any higher purpose other than the pure joy of simple existence? All of the expressions of life are celebrations of life, in the same way as a cook prepares a meal to celebrate a particular a special day. The cause and the effect of the meal are nothing but joy, the joy of the moment.

Chapter 3 Wisdom

1. You know the Self, by nature one without end. You know the Self, and you are serene. How can you still desire riches?

> You know that happiness is a state of mind, not a state of material things. Riches cannot give you contentment and peace. Contentment comes from being satisfied with who you are at the moment. Contentment is a state where there is no more lack in you.

2. When from ignorance you see silver in mother-of-pearl, greed arises. From ignorance of the Self desire arises for the world where the senses whirl.

> This world appears in you, the pure awareness. Attachment of this awareness to material objects causes you to feel the need for more of these objects. You cannot find satisfaction in more and more objects. You can only find satisfaction in more and more of yourself, pure awareness.

3. Knowing yourself as That in which the worlds rise and fall like waves in the ocean, why do you run about so wretchedly?

> Knowing that you are the limitless Self-awareness, you realize that the pursuit of material objects is like reaching for clouds in the sky. From a distance they look real, but when you grab them, there is nothing found inside your hand.

4. For have you not heard? You are pure awareness, and your beauty is infinite! So why let lust mislead you?

> The pursuit of pleasure for pleasure's sake will get you nowhere but to a diminishing of your energy. You are wasting your time and money attempting to find contentment in ever more intriguing pleasures. You will not find peace in those, only exhaustion and fatigue.

5. The person who is wise knows him/herself in all things and all things in him/herself. Yet how strange! He/she still says, "This is mine."

> There is nothing personal in this world, and yet people proclaim: "this is mine and that is yours." This body of yours originated as a combination of your mother's and father's biological substances. There is nothing about this body that you can call "yours." The intelligence inside this body is not yours either. The children you bear are not yours; the house you live in does not belong to you, etc. Nothing is "yours" because when you entered this world you brought nothing with you and when you leave it you will take nothing with you. You are only a caretaker of certain aspects of this creation for a very limited period of time.

6. Determined to be free, he/she abides in the oneness beyond all things. Yet how strange! Indulging in passion, he/she weakens, and lust overwhelms him/her.

> Many have a desire to be free. But as soon as they sense the slightest amount of freedom, they run back to the comfort of restrictions. Old institutions are not given up, old customs are maintained, pleasures are not given up, and the truth is set aside because of a fear of change.

7. Feeble with age, still he/she is filled with desire, when without doubt he/she knows that lust is the enemy of awareness. Indeed, how strange!

> Holding on to the body until the very end of life, you give up your freedom in awareness and suffer needlessly. Pain and suffering spring from involvement with the body. You know that. So, why not give up the idea that you are the body and find yourself as pure awareness free from all pain?

8. He/she longs to be free. He/she has no care for this world or the next, and he/she knows what is passing or [what is] forever. And yet how strange! He/she is still afraid of freedom.

> To be open to the moment is to be in freedom. Restrictions based on memory hold you in a prison. Conscious acceptance of the moment is necessary for you to be free in awareness.

9. But he/she who is truly wise always sees the absolute Self. Celebrated, he/she is not delighted. Spurned, he/she is not angry.

> Nothing can imprison you when you do it with the right awareness. Coming from a place of witnessing dispassion while you are involved with

the world will set you free from entanglements with the world.

10. Pure of heart, he/she watches his/her own actions as if they were another's. How can praise or blame disturb him/her?

> Life appears like a drama to you in which you are both the inactive witness and the active performer. You may be engaged in activities, but you are also the silent witness behind these activities.

11. With clear and steady insight he/she sees this world is a mirage, and he/she no longer wonders about it. How can he/she fear the approach of death?

> "Is this world real or unreal?" Such questions become irrelevant to you when you see that all is taking place in your awareness alone. Awareness alone is real. This world is a reflection appearing in awareness. All objects are reflected in awareness, including your body. Attachment to your body creates fear of death. Seeing your body in your witnessing awareness creates freedom from this fear of death.

12. Pure of heart, he/she desires nothing, even in despair. He/she is content in the knowledge of the Self. With whom may I compare him/her?

> Being content within your own Self, there is nothing that you need in order to be. In a materialistic society many artificial needs are created which cause confusion in you. Happiness,

peace and contentment are not dependent on material things. They come when you see yourself as you truly are: unlimited awareness.

13. With clear and steady insight he/she knows that whatever he/she sees is by its very nature nothing. How can he/she prefer one thing to another?

> Material things cannot add to your happiness or to your sense of being. Whether you possess a piece of gold or a piece of rock, they cannot add to you as pure awareness. You are what you are either with material possessions or without them. You as the pure Self-awareness do not change.

14. He/she is beyond all duality. Free from desire, he/she has driven from his/her mind all longing for the world. Come what may, joy or sorrow, nothing moves him/her.

> You are untouched by all of duality, the pair of opposites that exists in this material world. For every quality there is an opposite quality. Duality means that in order for you to be happy you must also experience the pain of unhappiness, etc. When you are the witness of duality, how can you suffer?

Chapter 4 The True Seeker

1. The wise person knows the Self, and he/she plays the game of life. But the fool lives in the world like a beast of burden.

> When the true Self is known, there is nothing else to be achieved in this life. Life itself requires that you act in certain situations, and you will do these acts. There is no more sense of individual doership in you and you will see your chores as part of the game of life. As long as you believe to be the doer of any act, you will suffer hardships in life.

2. The true seeker feels no elation even in that exalted state which Indra and all the gods unhappily long for.

> Contentment and peace are experienced in pure Self-awareness. Nothing else can bring about these feelings in the same way, not even the greatest riches, most treasured desires, hopes, dreams, aspirations. Nothing but the stillness of pure awareness can bring about real peace of mind.

3. He/she understands the nature of things. His/her heart is not smudged by right or wrong, as the sky is not smudged by smoke.

> What is the nature of things? They are a reflection in awareness. This becomes your strong conviction. Involvement with material things and feelings is cut down to a bare minimum. Awareness of the moment prevails in you most of the time.

4. He/she is pure of heart; he/she knows the whole world is only the Self. So, who can stop him/her from doing as he/she wishes?

> Expressing the love of your heart. Seeing this love reflected in all of creation. Such will be your life. You will ask "where is there another?" You will not be able to see another, since all takes place in your Self alone.

5. Of the four kinds of being [flying, swimming, walking, plants], from Brahma to a blade of grass, only the wise man or woman is strong enough to give up desire and aversion.

> Natural dispassion arises in you when pure Self-awareness is realized as the core of your being. What could you gain from acquiring different objects? What could you gain by rejecting various objects?

6. How rare he/she is! Knowing he/she is the Self, he/she acts accordingly and is never fearful. For he/she knows he/she is the Self, one without two, the Lord of all creation.

> You are the Self. What more can be said! You are the witness behind all that can be seen and experienced. You are pure love, pure awareness, pure bliss. You are the timeless presence. You cannot be adequately described. You are the source of all that exists. Awareness is the foundation of existence. You are this foundation.

Chapter 5 Dissolving

1. You are pure. Nothing touches you. What is there to renounce? Let it all go, the body and the mind. Let yourself dissolve.

> Enter into pure awareness. Be who you really are. Let go of all notions of being anyone or anything. Even the most exalted notion of yourself is limiting you. You can only be free when you have realized that you are unlimited awareness.

2. Like bubbles in the sea, all the worlds arise in you. Know you are the Self. Know you are one. Let yourself dissolve.

> Every thought, every feeling, all sights and sounds originate in you. When there is only one, why do you believe there are two? When you hurt someone else, it is you who suffers. When you make someone happy, it is you who feels happiness. Understand that you are the one Self in which all takes place.

3. You see the world. But like the snake in the rope, it is not really there. You are pure. Let yourself dissolve.

> When there is darkness, it is possible to mistake a piece of rope for a snake. The fear you experience is real, but the snake is not. As soon as you realize your mistake, your fear vanishes. This is analogous to seeing the world as the world and not as a reflection in awareness. The world cannot exist outside of awareness.

4. You are one and the same in joy and sorrow, hope and despair, life and death. You are already fulfilled. Let yourself dissolve.

> Nothing can add to your joy and happiness. You are the pure Self, full of bliss. Don't let someone tell you that you are limited. You are not limited; you are unlimited awareness, timeless and free. You are the witness of all, unencumbered and serene.

Chapter 6 Knowledge

1. I am boundless space. The world is a clay pot. This is the truth. There is nothing to accept, nothing to reject, nothing to dissolve.

> Whatever exists, exists in me. There is no other. The space inside a clay pot and the space outside of it are one and the same. All exists within me. I contain all the worlds.

2. I am the ocean. All the worlds are like waves. This is the truth. Nothing to hold on to; nothing to let go of; nothing to dissolve.

> I am infinite. This finite creation exists within me. Nothing is higher than me. Nothing is greater than me. I am the Alpha and Omega of existence.

3. I am the mother-of-pearl. The world is a vein of silver, an illusion! This is the truth. Nothing to grasp, nothing to spurn, nothing to dissolve.

> To see valuable silver in mother-of-pearl is an illusion. In the same way, to see the world as valuable is an illusion. The Self is all that exists. There is nothing higher or lower in the Self. Distinctions based on value or importance are nonexistent in pure Self-awareness.

4. I am in all beings. All beings are in me. This is the whole truth. Nothing to embrace, nothing to relinquish, nothing to dissolve.

> Whatever is in me, that is also in all others. All beings exist in my awareness, and my awareness exists in all beings. Awareness does not belong to "me" exclusively. Awareness belongs to all.

Chapter 7 The Boundless Ocean

1. I am the boundless ocean. This way and that, the wind, blowing where it will, drives the ship of the world. But I am not shaken.

> Nothing can touch me in my essence of pure Self-awareness. In my awareness I am completely still and unmoving. The qualities of body and mind go on with their merry game, but they cannot touch me at all. Deep down I am completely still and anchored safely.

2. I am the unbounded deep in whom the waves of all the worlds naturally rise and fall. But I do not rise or fall.

> Watching the play of the world, I am astonished at the multiplicity of this creation. So many thoughts, feelings, actions, forms, colors, sounds and sights! This play is performed at the surface of my being. Beyond this surface activity there is peace, calm and pure perceiving presence. Beyond this surface activity there is unmovingness.

3. I am the infinite deep in whom all the worlds appear to rise. Beyond all form, forever still. Even so am I.

> I support all of creation. In me alone does the world arise and subside. Thoughts and feelings originate in me and return to me. I am the witness and yet the creator of all. I am the witness but all I see is my own reflection in my pure and aware Self.

4. I am not in the world. The world is not in me. I am pure. I am unbounded. Free from attachment, free from desire, still. Even so am I.

> This world cannot touch me. I have no connection with the world. The world does not have me on its leash. I am free. Meditation on the Self has liberated my perception. Meditation on the Self has set me free. There is only one truth and that is the existence of the Self.

5. O how wonderful! I am awareness itself, no less. The world is a magic show! But in me there is nothing to embrace, and nothing to turn away.

> I am all alone inside my Self, yet I am never lonely. There is no other and I embrace myself constantly. Wherever I look there I see only myself reflected, yet I do not feel the need for another. I am satisfied being myself. My yearning has stopped, and I found myself.

Chapter 8 The Mind

1. The mind desires this, and grieves for that. It embraces one thing, and spurns another. Now it feels anger, now happiness. In this way you are bound.

> Attachment to the qualities of the mind causes pain. Do not get attached to them. See beyond them. Experience the bliss of pure awareness. Experience the pure witnessing awareness in which all the qualities of the mind are seen.

2. But when the mind desires nothing and grieves for nothing, when it is without joy or anger and, grasping nothing, turns nothing away. . . then you are free.

> Dispassion is the way to freedom from the qualities of the mind. Disinterest causes the strings of the mind's attachments to be cut. Dispassion and disinterest toward achievement in the material sphere are important in the struggle for freedom from the pull of constant desires.

3. When the mind is attracted to anything it senses, you are bound. When there is no attraction, you are free. Where there is no I, you are free.

> "I want this." Thinking like that will cause attachments to be formed. In reality there is no "I" and there is no "this." There is only the Self. Freedom from the bondage to sense pleasures is found in natural dispassion.

4. Where there is "I," you are bound. Consider this. It is easy. Embrace nothing, turn nothing away.

> Be who you are. Don't believe you can benefit from embracing certain sense pleasure, and don't believe you can benefit from rejecting certain sense pleasures. The senses only bring you information about the world. It is you who finds this information important enough to lose your sense of freedom. You want to get involved with sense objects. They look very enticing to you. But consider this: they are only a reflection in your own awareness. Other than this reflection in your Self, there is no reality to them.

Chapter 9 Dispassion

1. Seeing to this, neglecting that, setting one thing against another. . . who is free of such cares? When will they ever end? Consider. Without passion, with dispassion, let go.

> Why do you insist that one thing is more important than another? Constantly plotting to get the better of someone else, you are lost in divisions. Perceive all as expressions of the One and lead a life of deep peace and contentment.

2. My child, rare is he/she, and blessed, who observes the ways of people and gives up the desire for pleasure and knowledge, for life itself.

> What is there to attain, once the pure Self has been found? Where can you go to find more peace, more contentment, more joy, more bliss? In meditation on the Self all is found, all is accomplished, all is attained.

3. Nothing lasts. Nothing is real. It is all suffering, threefold affliction! It is all beneath contempt. Know this. Give it up. Be still.

> The origin of suffering is found in the three afflictions: notion of individual doership, notion of being a separate entity, and notion of incompleteness. All these afflictions are seen by awareness. They are not real because they vanish as soon as the truth is seen. Only awareness can exist on its own.

4. When will people ever stop setting one thing against another? Let go of all contraries. Whatever comes, be happy and so fulfill yourself.

> We all search for the Holy Grail. However, this Holy Grail is found only inside of us, at the source of our being, in pure awareness. Whatever we find in the external world has a beginning and an end. Nothing in this world is permanent. Why would you use this world as the corner stone of your search for happiness and peace?

5. Masters, saints, seekers: They all say different things. Whoever knows this, with dispassion, becomes quiet.

> The teachings of the highest truth about the Self are expressed differently by different teachers during different times and at different places. What is so astonishing about that? All teachings are designed for the students of the moment, not for another time or place. Words should not confuse you. The essence of the teachings about the Self point to peace of mind and nothing else.

6. The true master considers well. With dispassion, he/she sees all things are the same. He/she comes to understand the nature of things, the essence of awareness. He/she will not be born again.

> There is no need to run here or there in search of the Self. Wherever you are, there the Self can be found. The Self is with you all the time. The peace of the Self is accessible to you all the time. It is you who do not look within and experience the Self.

Focus your mind and see the stillness at the source of your mind.

7. In the shifting elements see only their pure form. Rest in your own nature. Set yourself free.

> All of nature changes constantly. Where is there stability in this creation? Where is there security in life? Somewhere there has to be a center, a foundation that can provide you with a place of certitude. This place is in awareness. This is your real nature. Here the fluctuations of life have no impact. Here you are safe from the battering storm of the elements.

8. The world is just a set of false impressions. Give them up. Give up the illusion. Give up the world. And live freely.

> What makes this world real? Only your experience of it makes it real. But where does this experience take place? In awareness! You may call it "your" awareness, but you cannot know "another" awareness. You exist as awareness, and you perceive all within you.

Chapter 10 Desire

1. Striving and craving for pleasure or prosperity, these are your enemies, springing up to destroy you from the presumptions of virtue. Let them all go. Hold on to nothing.

> What is the value of any material possession if it does not further the growth of your soul? Constantly strive toward the highest ideals of selflessness and perfection. Do not settle for the few crumbs of material comfort instead.

2. Every good fortune, wives, friends, houses, lands, all these gifts and riches. . . they are a dream, a juggling act, a traveling show! A few days, and they are gone.

> Is there anything in this world that lasts more than a short period of time? Empires rise and fall, fortunes are won and lost, and people are born and die. Where is there hope for you to find happiness and peace in all of this?

3. Consider. Wherever there is desire, there is the world. With resolute dispassion free yourself from desire, and find happiness.

> It is not the world that clings to you, but you who cling to the world in search for happiness. It is you who tries to squeeze joy out of rocks. Eventually you will see the uselessness of your attempts and you will turn away from finding happiness through material objects.

4. Desire binds you, nothing else. Destroy it, and you are free. Turn from the world. Fulfill yourself, and find lasting happiness.

> See clearly that you are only looking for satisfaction. Why are you looking for satisfaction? Because you believe you are lacking in satisfaction. You are not satisfied with your life now because you do not see that whatever is, is already perfect. You are perfect, this world is perfect, all your deeds are perfect and all that exists everywhere is also perfect. There is only perfection visible in existence. You must learn to see this perfection. Then you are truly satisfied all the time.

5. You are one. You are pure awareness. The world is not real. It is cold and lifeless. Nor is ignorance real. So, what can you wish to know?

> The world cannot give you more than what you have to offer to it. See it as the cause of suffering and you will suffer. See it as the cause of happiness and you will be happy. However, the world is not the cause of suffering or happiness. The world is as you see it because of your inner tendencies you are projecting onto the world. See the world as a reflection of your pure awareness and the world will be nothing but a reflection of supreme bliss and joy.

6. Life after life you indulged in different forms, different pleasures, sons and kingdoms and wives. Only to lose them all.

> Your relatives cannot give you happiness, your achievements cannot give you happiness,

nothing but the realization of yourself as pure awareness can give you happiness in life. You are wasting your time and energy trying to find contentment anywhere else but inside your Self.

7. Enough of the pursuit of pleasure, enough of wealth and righteous deeds! In the dark forest of the world what peace of mind can they bring you?

> Looking for another or something else outside of you leads to unhappiness and a restless mind. The grass always appears greener on the other side of some fence. And there are so many fences, and so little time! Stop swinging from tree branch to tree branch like a monkey looking for morsels of food. Become still within yourself and see pure awareness as your true inner Self.

8. How you have toiled, life after life, pressing into painful labor your body and your mind and your words. It is time to stop. Now!

> Relax! Enjoy the stillness of the mind. Some say that the Self lives between two thoughts, between two deeds, between the in-and outbreaths. However, the Self lies beneath all thoughts, beneath all deeds, and beneath all breaths. All activity exists on the surface of pure Self-awareness. All activity relates to the stillness of the pure Self-awareness in the same way as waves relate to the entire ocean. The ocean itself is unmoved in its depth by the play of the waves on its surface.

Chapter 11 Stillness

1. All things arise, suffer change and pass away. This is their nature. When you know this, nothing perturbs you, nothing hurts you. You become still. It is easy.

> What is coming and what is going? Is a flower dying or simply stepping aside to let another form of creation emerge? Where is there gain? Where is there loss? Only in your mind exists the perception of more or less, of higher or lower, of more important or less important. Beyond the mind, in pure awareness, no such distinctions exist. Here silence supreme reigns.

2. God made all things. There is only God. When you know this, desire melts away. Clinging to nothing, you become still.

> God is the highest, purest, eternal, limitless, and timeless. A portion of god resides in your body/mind structure as pure awareness. Your awareness is as pure as the awareness that dwells in all other body/mind structures in existence. Awareness is what connects all of creation. If you would not be aware of this creation, you would have no connection with it. Knowing that awareness underlies all, your search for satisfaction leads you to this awareness in still meditation. Meditation is the realization that awareness is the Self within you.

3. Sooner or later, fortune or misfortune may befall you. When you know this, you desire

nothing, you grieve for nothing. Subduing the senses, you are happy.

> The expressions of this creation are innumerable. There will always be new things that look tempting to you. However, the highest bliss that you can experience comes from knowing who you are: the pure Self deep within you which is commonly called awareness.

4. Whatever you do brings joy or sorrow, life or death. When you know this, you may act freely, without attachment. For what is there to accomplish?

> There will always be actions and subsequent reactions in this world. What is born will one day die, joy turns to sorrow, acceptance becomes rejection, etc. A win-win situation can only occur when you become the witness of both, positive and negative. It does not matter to you as awareness what you are aware of. Nothing can touch you in your purity of being.

5. All sorrow comes from fear. From nothing else. When you know this, you become free of it, and desire melts away. You become happy and still.

> Fear is based on memory. In the moment there is only wonder. When you face the moment with openness and disconnected from memory, then you are free from all influences of the past. Only then can you be the silent witness of life, the witnessing awareness that you fundamentally are.

6. "I am not the body, nor is the body mine. I am awareness itself." When you know this, you have no thought for what you have done or left undone. You become one, perfect and indivisible.

> All you have to accomplish in this life is to realize who you are: the pure Self that lives inside your body/mind as pure awareness. This realization is the apex of your existence. After this realization nothing more is needed for you to attain in order to live in happiness and peace. You cannot find happiness and peace in material objects; you can only find them in your Self.

7. "I am in all things, from Brahma to a blade of grass." When you know this, you have no thought for success or failure or the mind's inconstancy. You are pure. You are still.

> There is nothing higher in existence then your Self. All is seen in your Self-awareness. From the most significant aspect of creation to the most ordinary, all is contained within you.

8. The world with all its wonders is nothing. When you know this, desire melts away. For you are awareness itself. When you know in your heart that there is nothing, you are still.

> What is so special about this world? Whatever you perceive only comes to you by means of the senses. Whether you see a lump of gold or a lump of earth, the process is the same: you become aware of them. A value to these sense perceptions is put on by the mind, not by your awareness. Therefore,

how can anything be more valuable than something else to you, the pure witnessing awareness?

Chapter 12 Fulfillment

1. First I gave up action, then idle words, and lastly thought itself. Now I am here.

> I realized that I am not the doer. I realized that I am not my speech and not my mind. Who am I? I am the awareness witnessing it all.

2. Ridding my mind of distraction, single-pointed, I shut out sound and all the senses, and I am here.

> I have the will power to withdraw from the senses as well as from my thoughts and emotions. I am not attached to them any longer. Now I exist in utter freedom.

3. Meditation is needed only when the mind is distracted by false imagining. Knowing this, I am here.

> When I look around, all I see is a field of awareness. Thoughts arise in this field, and I am their witness. Emotions arise in this field, and I am their witness. This is the most pleasant state to be in.

4. Without joy or sorrow, grasping nothing, spurning nothing, O Master, I am here.

> My master has opened my eyes to the reality of my existence. He/she has told me that I am the Self, pure awareness. I have found out that he/she has told me the absolute truth. I am beyond all joy

and sorrow, beyond any lack, therefore not needing anything.

5. What do I care if I observe or neglect the four stages of life [student, householder, retired, renunciate]? Meditation, controlling the mind, these are mere distractions! Now I am here.

> What is the use of Mantras if I know who I am? Where can they lead me but to my own Self? There is no other. There is only the Self.

6. Doing, or not doing, both come from not knowing. Knowing this fully, I am here.

> I am neither the doer, nor am I the non-doer. Whether I act or do not act is the same to me. I do not run away from doing, nor do I run toward doing. Life itself causes me to act and life causes me not to act.

7. Thinking of what is beyond thinking is still thinking. I gave up thinking, and I am here.

> The mind is very limited in its understanding of my true nature. The mind wants to understand and label everything. However, the experience of the Self cannot be understood, one has to be it. The Self is awareness, while the mind=s activities are objects to this awareness. A mind itself does not exist, only the functions of the mind such as thoughts exist at certain times.

8. Whoever fulfills this fulfills his/her own nature and is indeed fulfilled.

> To know oneself is to know true happiness. The objective world cannot give this kind of pure happiness, only the spiritual world can do that. When you get in touch with the spirit within yourself, you will experience causeless bliss and causeless happiness.

Chapter 13 Happiness

1. Even if you have nothing, it is hard to find that contentment which comes from renunciation. I accept nothing. I reject nothing. And I am happy.

> Renunciation has only to do with the giving up of the erroneous notions of: I am the doer; I am separate; I am imperfect. After having given up these notions, there is no longer any need to give up anything else. Bliss and joy bubble up constantly after that.

2. The body trembles, the tongue falters, the mind is weary. Forsaking them all, I pursue my purpose happily.

> My goal is the attainment of the Self. Not knowing that I am the Self already, I seek myself in all kinds of venues. Now the body is exhausted from the many years of search; I lose my power of speech and my mind is beginning to leave me. And still I have not found my true Self. Where am I looking? Body/speech/mind cannot lead to my Self. Only the Self alone leads to the Self. My Self is pure awareness and bliss. Searching in awareness and bliss alone will make me find my Self.

3. Knowing I do nothing, I do whatever comes my way, and I am happy.

> As the witnessing awareness I am not involved in any action. Yet, my body and mind perform their assigned functions. I am the witness and I let body and mind be.

4. Bound to his/her body, the seeker insists on striving or on sitting still. But I no longer suppose the body is mine, or is not mine. And I am happy.

> Where can I go to find my Self? What can I do to uncover my Self? There is nowhere to go and nothing to do in this search. I am my Self here and now. Suppose some say that I should repeat the Mantra Shivo'Ham (I am Shiva, the Self). What is the purpose in that? Nobody points to a tree and keeps repeating: this is a tree; this is a tree. It is self-evident that I am the pure Self.

5. Sleeping, sitting, walking, nothing good or bad befalls me. I sleep, I sit, I walk, and I am happy.

> Observing all in complete silence, I am the blissful witness reflected in all. I see my Self reflected everywhere. I observe my mind and my body. I am not my mind or my body. I am hidden from them. They cannot reach me, nor can they know me. I, on the other hand know them fully. They cannot hide the smallest aspect from me. I know what the mind is thinking and feeling. I know what the body is sensing. Body and mind are my playgrounds.

6. Struggling or at rest, nothing is won or lost. I have forsaken the joy of winning and the sorrow of losing. And I am happy.

> Too many times have I looked for happiness in successes and achievements. What have they brought me? Only short-lived gratification. Now I have found true happiness in my Self and have lost the taste for other attainments. Nothing I do can

touch me as deeply as the realization that I am the pure and blissful Self. Therefore, my search for happiness has ended the moment I realized my inner Self.

7. For pleasures come and go. How often I have watched their inconstancy! But I have forsaken good and bad, and now I am happy.

> There is no end to sense pleasures. What was sufficient today is insufficient tomorrow, and so on. The mind wants more and more, better and better, prettier and prettier, tastier and tastier things. In the end the mind cannot be satisfied. In the end the mind will experience disappointment. Therefore, it is better to give up the drive for more and more pleasures and come to one's senses. Time and circumstances will make you renounce pleasure. Give them up now and find bliss in your inner Self, your own inner awareness.

Chapter 14 The Fool

1. By nature my mind is empty. Even in sleep, I am awake. I think of things without thinking. All my impressions of the world have dissolved.

> My awareness flows constantly, like a smooth-running river. There is stillness in me. Where is my mind? Where are my thoughts? I have lost interest in them. I have found satisfaction in my Self.

2. My desires have melted away. So, what do I care for money or the thieving senses, for friends or knowledge or holy books?

> Nothing holds any interest for me but my own Self. I experience my own Self as the only presence in existence. Where are there any "others?" The sense objects cannot steal away my stillness and peace any longer.

3. Liberation, bondage, what are they to me? What do I care for freedom? For I have known God, the infinite Self, the witness of all things.

> Liberation and bondage are only concepts of the mind. What I am is beyond liberation and bondage. I am pure awareness, unlimited and blissful. I have overcome the limiting concept of God and found my Self as the only being in existence.

4. Without, a fool. Within, free of thought. I do as I please, and only those like me understand my ways.

> My interests do not lie with material things. My interests do not lie with spiritual things. My interests lie nowhere. How can one live like this? This is the fool's way. No interest in anything other but my own inner stillness.

Chapter 15 The Clear Space of Awareness

1. The person who is pure of heart is bound to fulfill him/herself in whatever way he/she is taught. A worldly person seeks all of his/her life but is still bewildered.

> Seek the knowledge that can liberate you from attachments to this world. Do not seek knowledge that binds you more and more to this world. Seek the highest, not the higher or the lower. Seek the purest, not the pure or the impure. This will lead you to your own pristine Self.

2. Detached from the senses, you are free. Attached, you are bound. When this is understood, you may live as you please.

> Do you want to be free from all attachments and live in inner peace? Or do you wish to be attached to material things and live a life of pleasures followed by sorrows? The choice is yours. Renounce temptation, hopes, dreams, aspirations, and become still in your Self.

3. When this is understood, the person who is bright and busy and full of fine words falls silent. He/she does nothing. He/she is still. No wonder those who wish to enjoy the world shun this understanding!

> You cannot lead others in their quest for world domination once you have understood the truth about the existence of the pure Self as the source of all. All egotistic tendencies are burned up by the emergence of the pure Self-awareness.

Worldly people do not listen to the quiet whispers of their own inner Self. They are too busy piling up more and more material valuables so that they can appear to be content. Let them be. Sooner or later their house of cards will crumble, and their pain will be great.

4. You are not your body. Your body is not you. You are not the doer. You are not the enjoyer. You are pure awareness, the witness of all things. You are without expectation, free. Wherever you go, be happy!

> This world is the Garden of Eden. You entered it with nothing to call your own and you will leave it with nothing to call your own. So, why do you have to fight over the toys that have been provided for you? Is there not enough to go around so that all can live comfortably? Why do so few must have so much and so many have so little? What are your real needs? What are your overblown needs?

5. Desire and aversion are of the mind. The mind is never yours. You are free of its turmoil. You are awareness itself, never changing. Wherever you go, be happy.

> Happiness cannot come from involvement in attachment and aversion. Only unhappiness and dissatisfaction can come from it. What are the values of attachment and aversion? They have no value; they are truly worthless. They cause more harm than good. So, get rid of them once and for all. Bliss is only found in the space between attachment and aversion, in the space between joy and sorrow,

in the space between remembrance and hope. Bliss is experienced in the present, in the moment itself, in the absence of attachment to body, senses and mind.

6. For see! The Self is in all beings, and all beings are in the Self. Know you are free, free of "I," free of "mine." Be happy.

> Be who you are. You are pure awareness, the witnessing Self of all. If that is who you are, then why do you constantly try to find your Self in all kinds of activities? Many temptations beckon, but the Highest you will ever be able to experience is the bliss of your Self. So, give up the search for "more" and "better" and enjoy the still presence of your own Self.

7. In you the worlds arise like waves in the sea. It is true! You are awareness itself. So free yourself from the fever of the world.

> Give up running around frantically, trying to find happiness in this world. You will not find it. You can only be it. You are what you are looking for: peace, stillness, joy, bliss. Nothing originates outside of you. You are the beginning and the end of your existence. Only you exist. There is nothing else.

8. Have faith, my Child, have faith. Do not be bewildered. For you are beyond all things, the heart of all knowing. You are the Self. You are God.

> Where there is conviction, there is happiness. Where there is the truth, there is bliss. Only in spirit

is true happiness and bliss possible. Spirit is bliss. Spirit is happiness. Spirit is peace. What other god could possibly exist?

9. The body is confined by its natural properties. It comes, it lingers awhile, it goes. But the Self neither comes nor goes. So why grieve for the body?

> Awareness is the foundation of all that exists. You are this awareness. It is not "your" awareness dwelling in "your" body. It is awareness "of you" and "of your" body. This awareness does not distinguish between good or evil. That is the job of the mind. Awareness simply knows and sees all. Without awareness nothing is seen or known. Awareness is the eternal witness of all of existence.

10. If the body lasted till the end of time, or vanished today, what would you win or lose? You are pure awareness.

> Old age will not diminish you. Death has no meaning to you. You have never tasted death. Your mind experiences anguish at the thought of its demise and of the body=s. Gain and loss are the two ingredients that make up the game of life. How wonderful! There are constantly new forms. Old forms are the foundation of new forms. One form builds on another. All forms build an ongoing chain of the expressions of life. Become aware of the beauty and the magnificence of existence. You are much more than a body with a mind and a spirit. You are the witness of your body and mind.

11. You are the endless sea in whom all the worlds like waves naturally rise and fall. You have nothing to win, nothing to lose.

> You are unperturbed by the waves rising and falling. You enjoy their merry play. What is their purpose, you might ask? To celebrate life. To celebrate the existence of life! To celebrate your existence. Nothing else but you exist in this creation. Wherever you look, there you will find yourself reflected back at you. You are fulfilled in your own Self.

12. Child, you are pure awareness, nothing less. You and the world are one. So, who are you to think you can hold on to it, or let it go? How could you!

> What is transcendent? What is immanent? There is only you. How can you divide yourself into two or more? What part of you can pretend to be beyond the body, senses and mind? What part of you can pretend to be in the body, senses and mind? Those distinctions are utterly foolish. You are only one.

13. You are the clear space of awareness, pure and still, in whom there is no birth, no activity, no "I." You are one and the same. You cannot change or die.

> Be at peace always. Give up all fear of change. Give up all fear of uncertainties. Give up all worries about this and that. You are the pure Self, always blissful and fulfilled. You lack nothing. Nothing can be taken from you, and nothing can be added to you. You are satisfied.

14. You are in whatever you see. You alone. Just as bracelets and bangles and dancing anklets are all of the same gold.

> Look at the world. What do you see? Can you see the bliss that is reflected in the world? All sense organs bring impressions to your attention. Whatever comes before you causes bliss and joy in you. Whatever comes before you is recognized as your long-lost Self. "This is me!" "That is me!" "All there is, is only me!" "Is there no other?" "No, there is only myself, my own bliss and ecstasy!"

15. "I am not this." "I am He/She (God)." Give up such distinctions. Know that everything is the Self. Rid yourself of all purpose. And be happy.

> Do not run in this or that direction looking for happiness. The only direction you will find happiness in is the inner direction. Go within constantly. Give up all searches in all techniques. Find yourself in blissful awareness. All thoughts originate in bliss and merge into bliss. Follow your thoughts to this bliss. You are this bliss.

16. The world only arises from ignorance. You alone are real. There is no one, not even God, separate from yourself.

> There are no two. There is only one. How often must I say this? Listen, brother. You and I are one. Give up your sense of difference. Embrace yourself. Do not doubt that you alone exist. Like a turtle withdraw into your Self. Find your essence in yourself. Be yourself. Be pure awareness.

17. You are pure awareness. The world is an illusion, nothing more. When you understand this fully, desire falls away. You find peace. For indeed! There is nothing.

> Whatever you see, is seen in you, the pure awareness. You are not the mind, nor the body, nor a supposed ego. You are not separate from life. You are an integral part of life. As awareness you are the only one in existence. Nothing can exist outside of you. You are the Self of all. All is contained within you. What more do you want? The realization that you alone exist gives you supreme peace and contentment. This realization satisfies all your dreams and ambitions.

18. In the ocean of being there is only one. There was and there will be only one. You are already fulfilled. How can you be bound or free? Wherever you go, be happy.

> You are satisfied whether you move to the left or move to the right, whether you stand still or walk about, whether you meditate sitting or are active on your feet. Happiness is only one. Peace is only one. Contentment is only one. All is contained within you. Search for happiness, peace and contentment only inside of your Self.

19. Never upset your mind with yes and no. Be quiet. You are awareness itself. Live in the happiness of your own nature, which is happiness itself.

> "I want this." "I don't want that." Thoughts like these disturb your inner peace. Enjoy what

comes and enjoy what does not come. In the end all will be lost anyhow. What is the use of getting too involved with this world? You cannot create even a single blade of grass, so why do insist on collecting things and calling them "yours?"

20. What is the use of thinking? Once and for all, give up meditation. Hold nothing in your mind. You are the Self, and you are free.

> All thoughts appear in awareness. All mantras appear in awareness. If that is so, what is the purpose of repeating mantras and neglecting this awareness? Thoughts are ripples on the surface of awareness. Only awareness is free. Awareness is open to all. Thoughts are concentrated energies. Awareness is expanded energies. Be aware at all times. Awareness is freedom.

Chapter 16 Forget Everything

1. My child, you may read or discuss scripture as much as you like. But until you forget everything, you will never live in your heart.

> There is no end to scriptures. There is no end to discussions. Scriptures and discussions involve the mind. There is no end to the mind. All is seen in the pure Self-awareness. All ends in the Self. Where else can you find peace?

2. You are wise. You play, work, and meditate. But still, your mind desires that which is beyond everything, where all desires vanish.

> Give up looking for happiness and peace. Know that you are happiness and peace. You cannot find the peaceful Self in the outside world. The peaceful Self is revealed when your focus shifts from the outside to the inside.

3. Striving is the root of sorrow. But who understands this? Only when you are blessed with the understanding of this teaching will you find freedom.

> The craving for more and more is a cause of pain. The craving for less and less is also a cause of pain. Craving is the cause of pain. Craving leads the mind away from its peaceful center. Craving keeps you focused on something else, ignoring your inner Self.

4. Who is lazier than the master? He/she has trouble even blinking! But only he/she is happy. No one else!

> Nothing can be done in the pure state of Samadhi, the natural peaceful state. All is caused by the Self alone. No individual actions can take place. All actions based on individual desires come to a standstill. Only the universe flows on.

5. Seeing to this, neglecting that. . . But when the mind stops setting one thing against another, it no longer craves pleasure. It no longer cares for wealth or religious duties or salvation.

> The concept of "high" and "low" only exists in the mind. Life itself has no such distinctions. We humans are not the "masters" of this creation. We are not here to "subdue" this world. We are here to subdue the material desires in our minds, however. We are here to find peace and happiness despite our judgmental minds. We are here to realize the Self as the center of our being.

6. Craving the pleasures of the senses, you suffer attachment. Disdaining them, you learn detachment. But if you desire nothing, and disdain nothing, neither attachment nor detachment binds you.

> Let go of attachment and aversion. Neither one can set you free. Whether you love something intensely or hate it intensely, both emotions trap your mind into a state of restriction. Overwhelming feelings color your perception of the thing perceived. This coloring can cause delusion in your

perception of anything. Learn to see all objects, people, circumstances and events clearly.

7. When you live without discrimination, desire arises. When desire persists, feelings of preference arise, of liking and disliking. They are the root and branches of the world.

> To see something not clearly is the cause of delusion. Feelings can cloud your perception. Observe your feelings as well as the thing perceived, then you see with clarity more of the components of your perception. Look at life with an open mind. Do not shut any nuance of a perception out, including the perception of the perceiver, which is you. Be aware of all that creates a particular perception. The solution to any problem will make itself know in this way.

8. From activity, desire. From renunciation, aversion. But the man of wisdom is a child. He/she never sets one thing against another. It is true! He/she is a child.

> Find the middle ground in life. Not too much and not too little. Do not run after sense objects and do nor run away from sense objects. Stay in your center and life will give you what is rightfully yours.

9. If you desire the world, you may try to renounce it in order to escape sorrow. Instead, renounce desire! Then you will be free of sorrow, and the world will not trouble you.

> Who said that you must be poor in order to find happiness and peace? Who said that you must be wealthy in order to find happiness and peace? Only you know what is right for you. Do not lose your mental balance and clarity while being engaged in this world. Remain in your state of clarity, your state of clear Self-awareness and let life take care of your body, senses, mind and surroundings.

10. If you desire liberation, but you still say "mine," if you feel you are the body, you are not a wise person or seeker. You are simply a person who suffers.

> There is no going anywhere to find peace. There is no action you can do to attain peace. There is no other place or time than here and now to be in peace. There is no "over there" and there is no "over here." There is no "other" and there is no "me." There is only the Self. The Self is one. It cannot be divided into two or more parts. Parts only exist in the mind. Parts do not exist in pure awareness. Awareness cannot be divided into parts. Awareness can be aware of the parts shown by the mind.

11. Let Hari [Krishna] teach you or Brahma, born of the lotus, or Shiva himself! Unless you forget everything, you will never live in your heart.

> When someone teaches you, your mind generally forms concepts and beliefs based on these teachings. However, the truth is beyond concepts and beliefs. You have to let go of these concepts and beliefs in order to go beyond them to the state

of truth itself. These concepts and beliefs are floating on the surface of pure witnessing awareness. See them for what they are: thoughts in the mind, mixed with feelings. There may be a certain amount of fear to let go of your cherished ideas, concepts and beliefs, but you must in order to find freedom from them. Freedom cannot be found in limiting concepts and beliefs. Freedom is only found in the unlimited Self.

Chapter 17 Beyond All

1. The person who is happy and pure and likes his/her own company gathers the fruit of his/her practice and the fruit of wisdom.

> He/she lives in his/her own Garden of Eden, peaceful and content. He/she does not thirst for something other than what he/she has gained through his/her own efforts. He/she is self-contained. He/she has found the treasure of his/her inner Self. What more can a person want?

2. The person who knows the truth is never unhappy in the world. For he/she alone fills the universe.

> Once the truth about the Self is realized, no more lack is experienced. Where there is no more lack, there cannot be unhappiness. A self-satisfied person never lacks in happiness.

3. Just as the elephant loves the leaves of the sallaki tree, but not the neem tree, so the person who loves him/herself always spurns the senses.

> The contact with the inner Self causes contentment and deep peace. Contact with the senses causes turmoil and dissatisfaction. The better choice is obvious. Choose the Self and you will experience happiness and peace for as long as you shall exist.

4. It is hard to find a man or woman who has no desire for what he/she has not tasted, or who tastes the world and is untouched.

> The mind is constantly roaming the world looking for new excitements. This looking outside your Self for happiness causes an imbalance in your state of being. All your energies are outward directed. There is little energy left for introspection. To turn this habit around is not always easy. Sometimes life has to teach you a hard lesson about the futility of finding happiness in "others" and "other things."

5. Here in the world some crave pleasure, some seek freedom. But it is hard to find a man or woman who wants neither. He or she is a great soul.

> There are always people who indulge in one thing or another. Then there are always those people who are on some form of a diet or involved in some attempt to curb their cravings. Don't waste your energies with involvements or trying to overcome involvements. Be the witness of your life. Be aware of what you do and how what you do affects your body/mind. Find peace in your own Self, in your own company.

6. It is hard to find a man or woman who has an open mind, who neither seeks nor shuns wealth or pleasure, duty or liberation, life or death. . .

> What is the purpose of life? To celebrate life! Not to accumulate all kinds of wealth for the sake of possessing it, and not to search out every possible pleasure. We humans have the ability to go beyond

the mind to a state of pure awareness that is filled with bliss. If that is so, why are we still striving on the level of the mind for crumbs of happiness and morsels of peace?

7. He/she does not want the world to end. He/she does not mind if it lasts. Whatever befalls him/her, he/she lives in happiness. For he/she is truly blessed.

> Worldly oriented people do not want the world to end. They find many ways to extend the life of everything material, from their possessions to their own body. Billions of Dollars are spent every year in advanced countries on the search to prolong the life of this human body, while Millions of people die in underdeveloped countries because of a lack of food and lack of fundamental health care. "Everyone for him/herself." That is the motto of the selfish human mind. All will end eventually. So, why try to hold on to anything if you have to let go of it sooner than you think?

8. Now that he/she understands, he/she is fulfilled. His/her mind is drawn within, and he/she is fulfilled. He/she sees, and he/she hears, he/she touches and smells and tastes, and he/she is happy.

> Bliss is found within. Happiness is found within. Peace is found within. The senses play their merry game, but they cannot reach to the center of awareness. Nothing can add to your bliss, your happiness, your peace, neither can anything subtract from it.

9. Whatever he/she does is without purpose. His/her senses have been stilled. His/her eyes are empty. He/she is without desire or aversion. For him/her the waters of the world have all dried up!

> He/she enjoys life! What more can he/she do? There is no purpose to existence, other than to celebrate life, all of life, from the smallest to the highest. From a blade of grass to the magnificent sun. He/she wants nothing and rejects nothing. He/she becomes the innocent witness of all. He/she is constantly amazed at the variety of this creation. He/she does not see repetition around him/her. Every day is a new day. Every act is a new act. Every thought is a new thought. He/she lives in freedom from the influence of his/her memory.

10. He/she is not asleep. He/she is not awake. He/she never closes his/her eyes or opens them. Wherever he/she is, he/she is beyond everything. He/she is free.

> He/she is aware of his/her Self. He/she is only looking at the Self. Whether he/she is asleep or awake, his/her attention is on the Self. When he/she walks, he/she walks in the space of the Self. His attention is beyond wherever he/she is. He/she is seemingly in this world, but he/she is really beyond this world. He/she walks on the earth, but his/her attention is on the divine.

11. And the person who is free always lives in his/her heart. His/her heart is always pure. Whatever happens, he/she is free of all desires.

> He/she is unsullied by the influences of this world. He/she sits safely inside the Self while the tornado of life unleashes its fury upon his/her body, senses and mind.

12. Whatever he/she sees or hears or touches, whatever he/she smells or tastes, whatever he/she acquires, he/she is free. Free from striving, and from stillness. For indeed, he/she is a great soul.

> He/she knows that he/she is liberated, whether he/she enjoys his/her own inner stillness or is involved with activities. Nothing can disturb his/her inner peace. He/she loves all equally and rejects none. He/she is like the sun, whoever comes before him/her is equally welcome.

13. Without blame or praise, anger or rejoicing. He/she gives nothing. He/she takes nothing. He/she wants nothing, nothing at all.

> What is there for him/her to accept or to reject, since only he/she exists? Can he/she reject him/herself? Can he/she accept him/herself? Whom can he/she blame? Whom can he/she praise? Can a candle illumine the sun? Can a drop of water wet the ocean? He/she is fulfilled in his/her own Self. He/she is satisfied and at peace.

14. And whoever draws near him/her, a woman full of passion or Death Himself, he/she is not shaken. He/she stays in his/her heart. He/she is free indeed!

> Nothing can influence him/her. He/she is pure awareness itself. He/she is the witness of his/her

body, senses and mind. Untouched by all he/she resides in a place beyond body, senses and mind.

15. It is all the same to him/her. Man or woman, good fortune or bad, happiness or sorrow. It makes no difference. He/she is serene.

> The search for happiness in the external world has no meaning for him/her, since he/she found peace in the awareness of his/her pure Self. What is there for him/her to attain? Where is there for him/her to go? He/she is free, yet he/she restricts him/herself to the bliss of his/her own Self. The whole world is his/her playground, yet he/she finds the most pleasure in him/herself.

16. The world no longer holds him/her. He/she has gone beyond the bounds of human nature. Without compassion or the wish to harm, without pride or humility. Nothing disturbs him/her. Nothing surprises him/her.

> Whatever happens is welcome by him/her. Whatever does not happen is equally welcome by him/her. What does he/she desire? Only the peace of his/her own inner Self. What does he/she crave? The bliss of his/her own inner Self. What is he/she attracted to? The beauty of his/her own inner Self.

17. Because he/she is free, he/she neither craves nor disdains the things of the world. He/she takes them as they come. His/her mind is always detached.

> Love is always on his/her mind. He/she is saturated with divine love. Wherever he/she looks,

there he/she sees his/her own love reflected back at him/herself. He/she tells everyone to see only his/her own love everywhere. What else is there in life? Happiness comes from love. Peace comes from love. Joy comes from love.

18. His/her mind is empty. He/she is not concerned with meditation, or the absence of it, or the struggle between good and evil. He/she is beyond all, alone.

> His/her perception goes beyond the realm of duality. He/she sees all as expressions of awareness, of the pure awareness of his/her own Self. Immeasurable joy arises in him/her at this realization. He/she is satisfied with life. He/she is blissful. He/she lives beyond time and space as the witness in pure awareness.

19. No "I," no "mine." He/she knows there is nothing. All his/her inner desires have melted away. Whatever he/she does, he/she does nothing.

> The ocean of life has been calmed in him/her. No more waves, no more agitation, no more unrest. He/she is entirely at peace with him/herself. This state cannot be compared to any other state of the mind. This state is beyond the waking, dreaming and deep sleep states. This is the state of freedom from all. It is the state of pure love.

20. His mind has stopped working! It has simply melted away. . . and with it, dreams and delusions and dullness. And for what he/she has become, there is no name.

> Beyond the wall of the mind there is peace! There is bliss! There is unblemished happiness! Jump over this wall! Make the leap of faith! Throw yourself into pure awareness! Enjoy the bliss! Harvest the fruit of your search for happiness. Taste the mango of eternal love! Let yourself dissolve in the feeling of pure existence, of pure being, of the pure Self!

Chapter 18 The Master

1. Love your true Self, which is naturally happy and peaceful and bright! Awaken to your own nature, and all delusion melts like a dream.

> There is only one truth, and that is the truth of the Self. Only the Self exists. Nothing else. Find your Self. Love your Self. Find your own inner bliss and contentment. Nothing in the "outside" world can give you much satisfaction.

2. How much pleasure you take in acquiring worldly goods! But to find happiness you must give them all up.

> Sense pleasures will have to be given up at some point in your existence. Why not give up the desire for them now instead of waiting until they will be taken from you involuntarily? Happiness does not dwell in objects. Happiness dwells in your innocent mind.

3. The sorrows of duty, like the heat of the sun, have scorched your heart. But let stillness fall on you with its sweet and cooling showers, and you will find happiness.

> Give up looking for happiness in your job, in your activities, in your thoughts, even in relationships. Find your own happiness inside your Self. Only there can it be found in its fullest measure. Happiness from "others" is only a shadow of the pure happiness and bliss found inside you.

4. For the world is nothing. It is only an idea. But the essence of what is and of what is not can never fail.

> The objects of this world come and go. You cannot depend upon them at all. Do not rest your desire for happiness on them. You are pure awareness, the witness of all. If that is who you really are, why would you get involved in the game of duality where you are always depending on something else, or someone else for your happiness? Be who you are.

5. The Self is always the same, already fulfilled, without flaw or choice or striving. Close at hand, but boundless.

> You are the Self. You are pure witnessing awareness. Realize this fact. That is all you have to do in this world. Nothing else matters. Nothing else can bring you to your true Self but the realization that you are pure Self-awareness.

6. When the Self is known, all illusions vanish. The veil falls, and you see clearly. Your sorrows are dispelled.

> In the mind there is always the search for more or less, the worrying about this or that, the hope for a better tomorrow. In the Self there is always peace and tranquility. In the Self all your fears are dispelled, all your worries dissolved, all your desires fulfilled.

7. For the Self is free and lives forever. Everything else is imagination, nothing more!

Because the master understands this, he/she acts like a child.

> The Self is not bound by time. Time only exists for relative objects. Pure Self-awareness is beyond relativity. The Self is the witness of space and time, of objects and events. The Self does not age. The Self is ever young. The Self is ever innocent.

8. When you know you are God and that what is and what is not are both imaginary, and you are at last free of desire, then what is there left to know or to say or to do?

> You are the highest. You are the witness of all. You are the field in which creation unfolds. Allow life to go on without interfering in it and enjoy the outcome. Be at peace and know that you exist in total freedom.

9. For the Self is everything. When the seeker knows this, he/she falls silent. He/she no longer thinks, "I am this, I am not that." Such thoughts melt away.

> There is nothing else but reflections of and in awareness. You are this awareness. Your thoughts, deeds, emotions, hopes, dreams, all are reflections of you in your Self. You are the wave and the ocean. You are the raindrop and the river. You are the grain of sand and the entire beach.

10. He/she is still. Without pleasure or pain, distraction or concentration, learning or ignorance.

> Stillness of mind is attained when you realize that all that exists is the one Self-awareness. What more is there to strive for? What more can you hope to find? You are the Self, and all "others" are reflections of your very own Self.

11. His/her nature is free of conditions. Win or lose, it makes no difference to him/her. Alone in the forest or out in the world, a god in heaven or a simple beggar, it makes no difference!

> He/she is satisfied wherever he/she is. He/she does not hope for a better time or a better place. He/she has entered the sacred shrine of his/her own Self. He/she is fulfilled. Whether it is daytime or nighttime, he/she is the same Self.

12. He/she is free of duality. Wealth or pleasure, duty or discrimination means nothing to him/her. What does he/she care what is accomplished or neglected?

> There are so many do-gooders in this world. What do they really accomplish? Have they found lasting happiness? There are so many points of view in this world. Can all be right? Perhaps all are wrong? The love of the Self cleanses all motives and all points of view.

13. Finding freedom in this life, the seeker takes nothing to heart, neither duty nor desire. He/she has nothing to do but to live out his/her life.

> There is nowhere for him/her to go anymore. The whole world is the master's playground, but he/she restricts him/herself to the bliss of his/her

own Self. He/she does not go out looking for anything anymore. The master has found his/her life's treasure and it turned out to be his/her own inner Self.

14. The master lives beyond the boundaries of desire. Delusion or the world, meditation on the truth, liberation itself-- What are they to him/her?

> Equality is his/her vision. He/she has overcome the viewpoint of "high" and "low." All is the same to him/her. All of life's expressions are sacred to him/her. He/she honors all. Wherever the master is, there he/she is in the presence of the Divine.

15. You see the world and you try to dissolve it. But the master has no need to. He/she is without desire. For though he/she sees, he/she sees nothing.

> This world is between illusion and reality. It is neither entirely illusory, nor entirely real. For a person with correct vision, it is his/her own Self. For a person with faulty vision, it is something else.

16. When you have seen God you meditate on Him/Her, saying to yourself, "I am He/She." But when you are without thought and you understand there is only one, without a second, on whom can you meditate?

> There is only bliss swimming in bliss. There are no more forms or concepts to meditate on. They all have dissolved in bliss. Boundaries and obstacles have disappeared. Peace and tranquility have set in.

Awareness has become a still stream running steadily and harmoniously.

17. When you are distracted, you practice concentration. But the master is undistracted. He/she has nothing to fulfill. What is there left for him/her to accomplish?

> When your mind goes in a direction you do not want it to go, then you try to pull it back. That is concentration. But when you know that in every direction lies only your own Self, where can you pull back your mind to? Over here is your own Self, and over there is your own Self. Doing and not-doing occur in your own Self.

18. He/she acts like an ordinary man. But inside he/she is quite different. He/she sees no imperfection in him/herself, nor distraction, nor any need for meditation.

> The notion of "I am imperfect" has left him/her. The notion of "I am indeed perfect" has been established in him/her. He/she feels no lack, no desire for "more" or "less." He/she is satisfied within him/herself.

19. He/she is awake, fulfilled, and free from desire. He/she neither is nor is not. He/she looks busy, but he/she does nothing.

> He/she is like the still waters of the ocean. The rivers of sense perceptions run into the ocean but cannot disturb his/her stillness. He/she sits in his/her own perfection, in his/her own inner peace, protected from the turbulent waters of the world.

20. Striving or still, he/she is never troubled. He/she does whatever comes his/her way, and he/she is happy.

> His/her focus is always on the inner Self. All his/her endeavors originate in the inner Self and end in the inner Self. His/her only purpose is to celebrate the pure Self-awareness. In this, he/she finds supreme happiness.

21. He/she has no desires. He/she has cast off his/her chains. He/she walks on air. He/she is free, tumbling like a leaf in the wind, from life to life.

> Wherever life puts him/her, there he/she is satisfied. He/she wants neither to live nor to die. He/she lives beyond his/her body, senses and mind. He/she is the impartial witness of all.

22. He/she has gone beyond the world, beyond joy and sorrow. His/her mind is always cool. He/she lives as if he/she had no body.

> His/her attention is always on the Divine. He/she lives in the Divine. He/she is the Divine. Does the Divine experience joy and sorrow? Does the Divine have a body or mind? The Divine is beyond all experiences, beyond all form, beyond all manifestations.

23. His/her mind is cool and pure. He/she delights in the Self. There is nothing he/she wishes to renounce. He/she misses nothing.

> Yes, his/her mind is always a pure reflection of the Self. His/her only desire is for the upliftment

of all. He/she serves all. He/she has no desire for self-aggrandizing. He/she sees him/herself neither superior nor inferior to anything.

24. His/her mind is naturally empty. He/she does as he/she pleases. He/she is not an ordinary man. Honor and dishonor mean nothing to him/her.

> He/she is steady in him/herself. He/she does not run here or there when the senses beckon him/her. Through the power of discrimination, he/she has pierced the veil of duality. He/she knows the truth about life. He/she has found him/herself to be the center of existence.

25. "The body does this, not I. My nature is purity." With these thoughts, whatever he/she does, he/she does nothing.

> "If all that exists is only my own Self, how can anything I do or not do make any difference to me?" This is how the man and woman of knowledge feel about this existence.

26. But he/she pretends not to know. He/she finds freedom in this life, but he/she acts like an ordinary man. Yet he/she is not a fool. Happy and bright, he/she thrives in the world.

> The depth of a realized person cannot be understood by ordinary people. Therefore his/her achievement cannot be adequately explained to them. All have to make this journey to the Self alone. Only pointers and helpful hints can be given. Grace alone can lead a person to the liberated state. This grace happens in the moment itself. All

realizations happen in the moment. Gradual progress is not possible on the spiritual path. Either you have realized the truth, or you have not. There is no middle ground.

27. Weary of the vagaries of the mind, he/she is at last composed. He/she does not know or think, or hear or see.

> The mind sometimes thinks it has found the answer to the question: "Who am I?" However, the true answer can only come from clear and free Self-awareness. The mind is limited, while the awareness is unlimited. Only this unlimited awareness can know the truth about who you are.

28. Undistracted, he/she does not meditate. Unbound, he/she does not seek freedom. He/she sees the world, but knows it is an illusion. He/she lives like God.

> He/she sits, he/she observes, he/she enjoys. Life flows all around him/her. There is nothing other than this flow of life that he/she perceives. Things come and go. People come and go. He/she is the witness of all.

29. Even when he/she is still, the selfish man or woman is busy. Even when he/she is busy, the selfless man or woman is still.

> There is never a moment when the liberated person is without stillness. There is hardly ever a moment where the attached person is with stillness. Stillness are moments of grace which should be fully appreciated as gifts from God.

30. He/she is free. His mind is unmoved by trouble or pleasure. Free from action, desire or doubt, he/she is still, and he/she shines!

> He/she is the witness of the states of his/her mind. He/she is the witness of the sense perceptions of his/her body. He/she is the witness of the events shaping his/her life. He/she is like the sun witnessing everything and enjoying it all.

31. His/her mind does not strive to meditate or to act. It acts or meditates without purpose.

> What is there to attain if all is one's own Self? Whatever state he/she gets into, there is his/her own Self already present. The mind is a tool that follows the needs of the moment. If there is a need to act, then there is action. If there is a need for meditation, then there is meditation. There is no higher purpose than the need of the moment.

32. When a fool hears the truth, he/she is muddled. When a wise person hears it, he/she goes within. He/she may look like a fool, but he/she is not muddled.

> The ignorant suffers manifold. Even in the sight of the truth he/she is incapable of opening up to it. The ignorant is truly unfortunate. However, it is only the mind that stands in the way of the realization of the Self. The wise person's mind has become transparent, while the fool's mind remains clouded.

33. The fool practices concentration and control of the mind. But the master is like someone asleep.

He/she rests in him/herself and finds nothing more to do.

> "I must do this practice in order to attain the Self!" Thinking like this keeps the ignorant in the realm of duality. Beyond this realm of duality is the pure awareness of the Self. It is always accessible as soon as the notion of doership vanishes from one's mind.

34. Striving or still, the fool never finds peace. But the master finds it just by knowing how things are.

> Even in meditation, the ignorant cannot find rest because of identification with the tendencies of his/her mind and body. The wise person gives up this identification and lives in peace in his/her body and mind, allowing them to be.

35. In this world people try all kinds of paths. But they overlook the Self, the Beloved. Awake and pure, flawless and full, beyond the world.

> Often times the path to freedom is loaded with prescriptions and dogmas. How can freedom be found through restrictions? The Self is the witness behind the mind and waits impatiently to be discovered by the pure of heart and pure of mind.

36. The fool will never find freedom by practicing concentration. But the master never fails. Just by knowing how things are, he/she is free and constant.

> Peace is the ultimate goal of all spiritual practices. This cannot be attained by torturing the body and mind. Only by letting those be and becoming their witness can freedom be found.

37. Because the fool wants to become God, he/she never finds him/her. The master is already God, without ever wishing to be.

> It is the subtle intellect that is the Self. The ignorant searches in vain in the realm of duality for the Self. Understanding itself is the Self. Knowing itself is the Self. Awareness itself is the Self.

38. The fool has no foundation. Fretting to be free, he/she only keeps the world spinning. But the master cuts at its root, the root of all suffering.

> "I want to be free." Words like these portray the ignorant. However, at least they are actively searching for a way out of suffering. Many others are addicted to the pleasure of the senses and resist all suggestions to give them up. The master greets the senses with a warm welcome and then withdraws happily into the comfort of his/her own Self.

39. Because the fool looks for peace, he/she never finds it. But the master is always at peace, because he/she understands how things are.

> On the level of the mind, peace is never to be found. On the level of the pure Self-awareness, nothing but peace is found. Therefore, let the mind be and enjoy the purity of your innermost essence, pure awareness.

40. If a person looks to the world, how can he/she see him/herself? The master is never distracted by this or that. He/she sees him/herself, the Self that never changes.

> The reflection of the Self in the world is much muted. The reflection of the Self in the clear and open mind is very pure. Therefore, strive with deep sincerity for an open and unfurnished mind. Clear the mind of all obstacles and it will reflect the Self in all of its simplicity.

41. The fool tries to control his/her mind. How can he/she ever succeed? Mastery always comes naturally to the one who is wise and who loves him/herself.

> The mind cannot be controlled. Can a huge rock tumbling down a mountain be controlled? All that can be done is to step aside and let the mind be. There is no use in fighting against the tendencies of the mind. Observe and acknowledge them, honor them, give them the proper place in your life. Only then can your mind become your friend.

42. One person believes in existence, another says, "There is nothing!" Rare is the person who believes in neither. He/she is free from confusion.

> "Does this universe exist, or does it not exist?" Questions like these are useless since they cannot be answered by the mind with absolute certainty. There is only one certainty in existence and that is the existence of pure Self-awareness. "I know that I am." The Self is existence, consciousness and bliss.

43. The fool may know that the Self is pure and indivisible. But because of his/her folly, he/she never finds it. He/she suffers all his/her life.

> Knowledge of the Self without the experience of the Self is of little use. The experience of the Self alone without knowledge of the Self is also of not much use. Knowledge and experience of the Self combined results in freedom from the mind and ego.

44. The mind of a person who longs to be free stumbles without support. But the mind of someone who is already free stands on its own. It is empty of passion.

> Without a strong guide, a person has a very difficult time on the path of freedom. Therefore, seek a Guru who has traveled the path and found the ultimate peace in pure Self-awareness.

45. The senses are tigers. When a timid man catches sight of them, he/she runs for safety to the nearest cave, to practice control and meditation.

> You cannot shut out the senses forever. Therefore, become the friend of your senses. Let them show you the world, and then move your mind to the side so that you can see the world in its intended beauty and magnificence.

46. But a person without desires is a lion. When the senses see him/her, it is they who take flight! They run away like elephants, as quietly as they can. And if they cannot escape, they serve him/her like slaves.

> Sense pleasures only provide a service as long as there is the notion of incompleteness to be found in the mind. Sense pleasures attempt to fill the lack of happiness that is felt in the mind. Pure Self-awareness on the other hand fills all emotional and psychological "black holes" in you and establishes supreme peace and happiness in your mind.

47. A person who has no doubts and whose mind is one with the Self no longer looks for ways to find freedom. He/she lives happily in the world, seeing and hearing, touching and smelling, and tasting.

> Freedom is a matter of day-to-day experience for a Self-realized person. Peace and happiness are day-to-day experiences of such a person. Stillness is his/her homeground.

48. Just by hearing the truth he/she becomes spacious and his/her awareness pure. He/she is indifferent to striving or stillness. He/she is indifferent to his/her own indifference.

> He/she can detect the truth in all teachings and all places. He/she does not shun the truth simply because it is espoused in a different place and a different form. Truth is the essence of all teachings. He/she is in tune with this truth.

49. The master is like a child. He/she does freely whatever comes his/her way, good or bad.

> The master is free from the consequences of his/her actions. He/she knows that only the three

tendencies [Gunas] of Sattva, Rajas and Tamas are acting in this world. He/she is unattached to them.

50. By standing on his/her own, a person finds happiness. By standing on his/her own a person finds freedom. By standing on his/her own, he/she goes beyond the world. By standing on his/her own, he/she finds the end of the way.

> Disinterested in all, a person of composure does not depend on anything else for support but his/her highest Self.

51. When a person realizes he/she is neither the doer nor the enjoyer, the ripples of his/her mind are stilled.

> Peace settles in when the witness of the doer and the enjoyer is revealed. This witness is the unattached Self.

52. The master's way is unfettered and free of guile. He/she shines. But for the fool there is no peace. His/her thoughts are full of desire.

> The master lives in freedom amongst the three Gunas. But the ignorant is thrown about and eventually swallowed up by them.

53. The master is free of his/her mind, and his/her mind is free. In this freedom he/she plays. He/she has a wonderful time! Or, he/she withdraws and lives in a mountain cave.

> Any place this master finds him/herself at becomes his/her playground. He/she is the center of the Universe.

54. If the master encounters a king or a woman or someone he/she dearly loves, he/she is without desire. And when he/she honors a god or a holy place or a person versed in the scriptures, there is no longing in his/her heart. None at all!

> Jealousy, infatuation, and envy do not exist in the mind of the master; neither does hope for a better tomorrow. The master is satisfied in the moment. He/she is at peace with him/herself.

55. He/she is unperturbed even when his/her servants despise him/her; or his/her wives, sons, and grandsons mock him/her. Even when his/her whole family makes fun of him/her, he/she is undismayed.

> The slaves to the world do not want to escape from the snares of this world and will stop others from achieving freedom as well. They are afraid of the sudden void in their lives and therefore do not like change. Those seeking freedom are often ridiculed by those stuck in outdated traditions and misguided beliefs.

56. For him/her there is no pain in pain, no pleasure in pleasure. Only those who are like him/her can know his/her exaltation.

> When the freedom in the Self has been found, there is no other state like it. This state is beyond pain, beyond pleasure. It is the highest state possible. It is a state of pure and blissful awareness.

57. He/she has no form. His/her form is emptiness. He/she is constant and pure. He/she has no sense of duty, which only binds people to the world.

> Once the highest and most natural state has been realized, there is no place or time where this state cannot be found. The Self is existence, consciousness and bliss. Can the Self have a form or a color or an odor or a taste that is distinct from any other form, color, odor, or taste?

58. The master fulfills his/her duties and is always untroubled. The fool does nothing and is always troubled and distracted.

> Whatever needs to be done will be done by the master. However, there is not very much that really needs to be done. Much of what the ignorant are engaged in on a daily basis is pure waste of time and energy. The search for happiness in the material world leads many astray.

59. The master goes about his/her business with perfect equanimity. He/she is happy when he/she sits, happy when he/she talks and eats, happy asleep, happy coming and going.

> The master has conquered the sense of urgency that many people are feeling. This sense of urgency makes people act impulsively and irrationally. Often people are running frantically from here to there not knowing the reasons why.

60. Because he/she knows his/her own nature, he/she does what he/she has to without feeling

ruffled like ordinary people. Smooth and shining, like the surface of a vast lake. His sorrows are at an end.

> He/she knows that the ultimate goal of all endeavors is the attainment of the pure inner Self. However, the Self is already attained. Therefore, the awareness of this already attained Self is the true goal of all endeavors. This can be achieved while sitting, walking, laying down or while being engaged in one's daily activities.

61. The fool is busy even when he/she is still. Even when he/she is busy the master gathers the fruits of stillness.

> The mind of the ignorant is not under his/her control. He/she has no power to stop the thoughts in his/her mind. In meditation, he/she is constantly trying to chase away his/her thoughts only to see them return with company and renewed strength. The ignorant has yet to learn that he/she is the witness of his/her thoughts, and that his/her thoughts are his/her very best friends.

62. The fool often spurns his/her possessions. The master is no longer attached to his/her body. So how can he/she feel attraction or aversion?

> To give up or not to give up? That is the question the ignorant struggles constantly with in his/her mind. One day he/she renounces everything, the next day he/she buys it all back because he/she misses his/her possessions. As long as this game is going on in his/her mind, true peace is impossible.

63. The awareness of the fool is always limited by thinking, or by trying not to think. The awareness of the person, who lives within, though he/she may be busy thinking, is beyond even awareness itself.

> "How can I find happiness?" Questions like these keep the ignorant in limitation. No redemption from limitations can occur as long as the ignorant beliefs him/herself to be a separate entity, separate from others, separate from the All.

64. The master is like a child. All his/her actions are without motive. He/she is pure. Whatever he/she does; he/she is detached.

> The master constantly perceives all in a new way. There is no repetition for the master. He/she experiences every moment in a new light. Because of that, he/she has no attachment to a previous moment. He/she is free from memory and repetition.

65. He/she is blessed. He/she understands the nature of the Self. His/her mind is no longer thirsty. He/she is the same under all conditions, whatever he/she sees or hears, or smells or touches or tastes.

> He/she is an expression of the pure Self, the pure awareness. He/she is free. He/she is beyond the senses and the mind. He/she is the witness of all. He/she knows that he/she is the Self.

66. The master is like the sky. He/she never changes. What does the world matter to him/her, or

its reflection? What does he/she care about seeking, or the end of seeking?

> The master has found the secret of life. He/she is the life itself. This life flows constantly. Any rock that obstructs this flow will be washed away by the current of life. The master's physical, mental and emotional tendencies are used as tools to clear the path of life for all.

67. He/she is ever the same. The victory is his. He/she has conquered the world. He/she is the embodiment of his/her own perfect essence, by nature one with the infinite.

> He/she has succeeded in detaching him/herself from the tendencies of this world. He/she lives as pure awareness in pure awareness. No sense pleasure has the power to involve him/her again into this ephemeral world.

68. What more is there to say? He/she knows the truth. He/she has no desire for pleasure or liberation. At all times, in all places, he/she is free from passion.

> The master lives in love, breathes in love, thinks about love, and speaks with love. Sometimes the master has to confront deep seated attachments through strong words and actions, but all is motivated by the deepest love and respect for life.

69. He/she has given up the duality of the world, which arises with the mind and is nothing more than a name. He/she is pure awareness. What is there left for him/her to do?

> All the master can do is helping those who come before him/her in search of liberation. His/her methods may vary from those of other masters, but the result will be the same, if the student is able to stay the course.

70. The man or woman who is pure knows for certain that nothing really exists; it is all the work of illusion. He/she sees what cannot be seen. His/her nature is peace.

> All is seen in the pure awareness that is the pure Self. If that is so, then what is this world that is seen? Only likes can perceive and interact with likes. Therefore, whatever is seen and perceived is nothing but pure awareness itself.

71. He/she does not see the world of appearances. So, what do rules matter to him/her, or dispassion, renunciation, and self-control? His/her form is pure and shining light.

> Whatever is seen is pure awareness, not the world of duality and differences. Where does such a man or woman walk, sit, drink, eat or sleep? All takes place in pure awareness alone.

72. He/she does not see the world. So, what does he/she care for joy or sorrow, bondage or liberation? He/she is infinite and shining.

> The world has lost its value to him/her. He/she is content in his/her own Self. Talk of liberation or bondage has no more meaning to him/her. He/she sees liberation in bondage and bondage in liberation.

73. Before the awakening of understanding, the illusion of the world prevails. But the master is free of passion. He/she has no "I," he/she has no "mine," and he/she shines!

> "Where has the ego gone?" Observations like these make the realized person find peace in him/herself.

74. He/she sees that the Self never suffers or dies. So, what does he/she care for knowledge or the world? Or the feeling "I am the body. The body is mine?"

> "Who am I?" This question is answered by the wise person as: "I am." The question is the answer, and the answer is the question.

75. The moment a fool gives up concentration and his/her other spiritual practices, he/she falls prey to fancies and desires.

> As long as one follows the letter of the prescriptions to liberation, one is bound by the circumstances of one's life. As soon as one follows the spirit of these prescriptions, then liberation comes rather quickly.

76. Even after hearing the truth, the fool clings to his/her folly. He/she tries hard to look calm and composed, but inside he/she is full of cravings.

> Only the realization of pure awareness in the moment brings freedom in awareness. Whatever is going on in the mind, such as concepts or beliefs,

has no value in realizing the pure natural state of awareness.

77. When the truth is understood, work falls away. Though in the eyes of others the master may seem to work, in reality he/she has no occasion to say or to do anything.

> The truth is that all takes place in awareness alone. Whether one works or does not work has no meaning at all. The universe needs to be maintained however, and therefore much needs to be done at times to accomplish that.

78. He/she has no fear. He/she is always the same. He/she has nothing to lose. For him/her there is no darkness, there is no light. There is nothing at all.

> There is nothing at all, but him/herself. That is the realization of the liberated person. Whatever he/she looks at, he/she knows that it takes place in him/her alone.

79. He/she has no being of his/her own. His nature cannot be described. What is patience to him/her, or discrimination or fearlessness?

> His/her individual self has merged with the universal Self. His/her individual will no longer has the power to negate the will of the universal Self. Whenever desires emerge in his/her mind that are contrary to the needs of the universe, they will be eradicated instantly.

80. In the eyes of the master, there is nothing at all. There is no heaven. There is no hell. There is no such thing as liberation in life. What more is there to say?

> There is only being. There is only the one Self in existence. The master has realized his/her identity with this Self. Heaven and hell, as well as liberation are states of the mind. Beyond the mind there is only pure Self-awareness.

81. Nothing he/she hopes to win. Nothing he/she fears to lose. His/her mind is cool and drenched with nectar.

> In the same way as the sun is rising and setting, so he/she conducts his/her life. He/she arises in the morning and eventually retires in the evening. Unattached to all he/she sleeps soundly and peacefully. The attached man or woman tosses and turns all night, burning with desire and plotting for his/her eventual victory.

82. Free from desire, he/she neither praises the peaceful nor blames the wicked. The same in joy and sorrow, he/she is always happy. He/she sees there is nothing to do.

> He/she loves all equally. What can he/she gain if all is seen as his/her own Self? "Brothers and sisters," he/she says, "we are all equals in this world."

83. He/she does not hate the world. He/she does not seek the Self. He/she is free from joy and sorrow. He/she is not alive, and he/she is not dead.

> He/she exists. He/she does not ask whether this world is real or unreal. He/she enjoys the wonders of this creation without falling into the trap of the notion of individual doership.

84. He/she is not attached to his/her family. Free from the desire of the senses, he/she does not care about his/her body. The master expects nothing, and he/she shines.

> The master is pure. He/she is magnificent. He/she is a reflection of the Highest. The presence of the master bestows peace of mind. Such a master should be praised and honored.

85. Whatever befalls him/her, he/she is always happy. He/she wanders where he/she will. And wherever he/she finds him/herself when the sun sets, there he/she lies down to rest.

> His home is wherever he/she happens to live. Whatever the tendencies of his/her mind are, so are his/her surroundings. Are the tendencies more sattvic, more rajasic, or more tamasic? His external life will reflect these tendencies.

86. He/she does not care if the body lives or dies. He/she is so firmly set in his/her own being that he/she rises above the round of birth and death.

> He/she has risen above body-consciousness. He/she is identifying with pure Self-awareness. The Self is all he/she knows, smells, hears, touches, feels and tastes. His/her mind has overcome the adversities and temptations of the world of duality.

87. He/she is full of joy. Attached to nothing, free from possessions, he/she stands on his/her own. His/her doubts dispelled, he/she wanders where he/she will, never setting one thing against another.

> He/she is free. He/she is his/her own master. He/she understands the workings of the mind. He/she is no longer confused as to his/her true identity.

88. The master shines. He/she never says "mine." Gold, stone, and earth -- They are all the same to him/her. He/she is not bound by sloth, nor consumed by his/her own activity. He/she has severed the knots which bind his/her heart.

> He/she has overcome the mental tendencies such as Tamas (sloth), and Rajas (activity). He/she has freed him/herself from these tendencies. They have become his/her friends and supporters.

89. Who can compare with him/her? Indifferent to everything, he/she is happy, and he/she is free. There is not the least desire in his/her heart.

> His heart is completely free of desires. That is something many of the people around him/her do not understand. After all, the wanting of more is accepted by most as the natural way of the world.

90. Only the person without desire sees without seeing, speaks without speaking, and knows without knowing.

> There is no more agent to the faculties of seeing, speaking and knowing. The eyes, the mouth and the mind become simple instruments of life.

91. In his/her view of things good and evil have melted away. A king or a beggar, whoever is free from desire shines!

> He/she has seen the light at the end of the tunnel. In fact, he/she is the light at the end of the tunnel. He/she is no longer the person, but an embodiment of awareness.

92. He/she is utterly without guile. He/she has found his/her way. He/she is simplicity itself. He/she cares nothing for restraint, or abandon. He/she has no interest in finding the truth.

> If he/she would be asked: "What is the purpose of existence?" he/she would laugh and turn his/her back on the questioner. In silence he/she would sit, totally absorbed in his/her inner Self.

93. He/she has no desires. He/she rests happily in the Self. His sorrows are over. How can anyone tell what he/she feels inside?

> With every gesture and word, he/she points to the inner Self. Even in silence, he/she shows us the way to the Self. Follow such a master until he/she reveals the mystery of life to you.

94. Even when he/she is sound asleep, he/she is not asleep. Even when he/she is dreaming, he/she does not dream. Even when he/she is awake, he/she

is not awake. Step by step, whatever befalls him/her, he/she is happy.

> He/she is not the mind, nor the states of consciousness as reflected in the mind. He/she is beyond the mind as pure witnessing awareness. This is hard to understand by people who try to explain everything with language based on words based on letters based on sounds. The Absolute is beyond sounds.

95. He/she thinks without thinking. He/she feels without feeling. He/she is intelligent, but he/she has no mind. He/she has personality, but with no thought for him/herself.

> The three Gunas: Sattva (purity), Rajas (activity) and Tamas (inertia) act out their play in this world through him/her. He/she is the witness of this play. Sometimes one or the other Guna dominates his/her actions. This can cause happiness or friction in his/her surroundings. He/she is not the doer of these actions, and no residue will attach itself to him/her when the action is over.

96. He/she is not happy, nor is he/she sad. He/she is not detached, nor is he/she bound. He/she is not free, nor does he/she seek freedom. He/she is not this. He/she is not that. (Neti-neti).

> He/she lives on the fine line between attachment and aversion, between becoming and what has been, between tomorrow and yesterday. He/she lives in the moment. Because he/she lives in the moment, he/she is free from the past and free from the future.

97. Amid distractions, he/she is undistracted. In meditation, he/she does not meditate.
Foolish, he/she is not a fool. Knowing everything, he/she knows nothing.

> He/she is a puzzle even to him/herself. Does he/she know, or does he/she not know? He/she is established in the Self. That is all he/she knows. Everything else comes to him/her only when necessary and when life dictates it.

98. He/she always lives within. He/she is everywhere the same. Action or duty is nothing to him/her. Because he/she is free from desire, he/she never worries about what he/she has done or has not done.

> Awareness is reflected as consciousness in the mind. When the mind becomes completely transparent, awareness and consciousness become identical. When this happens, total freedom from the states of the mind is experienced.

99. Blame does not disturb him/her, nor does praise delight him/her. He/she neither rejoices in life, nor fears death.

> He/she has nothing to gain and nothing to lose. He/she has no stake in the outcome of any endeavor. In his/her view, life proceeds in a perfect and natural manner at all times.

100. His/her mind is calm. Never seeking the solitude of the forest, nor running from the crowd. Always and everywhere, he/she is one and the same.

> In the midst of a crowd and in the midst of the desert he/she is him/herself. He/she does not lose him/herself in the group psychology of large gatherings, nor does he/she lose him/herself when finding him/herself completely isolated from all.

Chapter 19 My Own Splendor

1. With the pincers of truth, I have plucked from the dark corners of my heart the thorn of many judgments.

> The light of the truth has shown into every corner of my being. There is no place in me where I hold anything back from the truth, from openness, from acceptance. This openness scts me free.

2. I sit in my own splendor. Wealth or pleasure, duty or discrimination, duality or non-duality, what are they to me?

> When it comes down to it, I am all alone in this world. Attachment to all has to be given up in the end, so why not give it up at this very moment?

3. What is yesterday, tomorrow, or today? What is space, or eternity? I sit in my own radiance.

> I am the eternal witness of the play of creation, sustenance and destruction. Why should I run hither and thither in the search for satisfaction? Why don't I simply make my stand right here, right now?

4. What is the Self, or the not-Self? What is thinking, or not thinking? What is good or evil? I sit in my own splendor.

> Discussions about "this" versus "that" are fruitless. The happiness I feel right now is real.

Concepts cannot explain what I feel. I am satisfied in my own being.

5. I sit in my own radiance, and I have no fear. Waking, dreaming, sleeping, what are they to me? Or even ecstasy?

> Whatever comes to me has a way of leaving me eventually. Should I search for happiness outside myself when I know for certain that whatever I find is short-lived?

6. What is far or near, outside or inside, gross or subtle? I sit in my own splendor.

> I am centered in my own being. I know my Self. I am happy. What more can I want?

7. Dissolving the mind, or the highest meditation, the world and all its works, life or death, what are they to me? I sit in my own radiance.

> When I go to the left, I only find myself there. When I go to the right, I equally find only myself there. When I go deep inside my mind during meditation, I find nothing but myself there. I cannot leave the area where I can be found, even if I tried.

8. Why talk of wisdom, the three ends of life [for a householder: Artha = private gains; Dharma = pursuit of religious duties; Kama = pursuit of pleasures], or oneness? Why talk of these! Now I live in my heart.

> Talk can only take place in the mind. The mind is limited in its expressions. I am the

awareness behind the mind. The mind can never express me adequately.

Chapter 20 I Am Shiva

1. I am fulfilled. The elements of nature, the body and the senses, what are they to me? Or the mind? What is emptiness or despair?

> I have renounced everything, including renunciation itself. I have found the inexpressible bliss at the center of my being.

2. What are holy books, or knowledge of the Self, or the mind, even when it is free of the senses? Or happiness, or freedom from desire? I am always One without two.

> There are many holy books, many paths to gain knowledge of the Self, many sense objects that entice the mind. All these many things cannot distract me from the simple fact that I am only one, that I am one without a second.

3. Knowledge or ignorance, freedom or bondage, what are they? What is "I," or "mine," or "this?" Or the form of the true Self?

> Yes, this creation exists. Yes, my body exists. Yes, my mind exists. All these are the forms of the Absolute. Awareness lives in all these forms as the pure and unattached witness.

4. I am always One. What do I care for freedom in life or in death, or for my present karma?

> Nothing can touch me in my essence as awareness. I am always free and pure. Try as I may

but contact with the body and mind has no effect on me in a negative or positive way.

5. I am always without I. So where is the one who acts or enjoys? And what is the rising or the vanishing of thought? What is the visible world, or the invisible?

> I am a single being. When I act, I divide myself into the one acting and the thing acted upon, as well as the task of acting. This is not easily understood, but it will become clear in time. In other words, I am all three parts of an action: the actor, the acted upon and the act itself.

6. In my heart I am One. What is this world? Who seeks freedom, or wisdom or oneness? Who is bound or free?

> Nothing gives me more pleasure than to find myself wherever I look. I see myself everywhere, from the highest to the lowest. That is the secret of this universe.

7. In my heart I am One. What is creation, or dissolution? What is seeking, and the end of seeking? Who is the seeker? What has he/she found?

> I may travel all over the world in search of happiness but will not find it outside myself. I may find different forms and colors, but the pure happiness and bliss I am capable of experiencing resides only in my Self.

8. I am forever pure. What do I care who knows, what is known, or how it is known? What do I care for knowledge? What do I care what is, or what is not?

> The highest is equally as important to me as is the lowest. Therefore, ignorance has equal value to me as knowledge. Gold is equal to clay. A diamond is equal to a piece of glass.

9. I am forever still. What are joy or sorrow, distraction or concentration, understanding or delusion?

> Living in peace is the highest goal one can attain in life. Peace within oneself, peace with one's neighbors, peace with all of one's surroundings. Peace based on inner stillness and complete Self-satisfaction.

10. I am always without thought. What is happiness or grief? What is here and now, or beyond?

> I am happy. I am at peace. I am aware of my Self.

11. I am forever pure. What is illusion, or the world? What is the little soul, or God himself?

> Untainted, stainless, pristine awareness. That is my nature. All is seen in awareness. How can anything be of greater value than something else? I have found the ultimate bliss at the core of my being.

12. One without two, I am always the same. I sit in my heart.

> What more can I desire? I am completely at peace, completely at ease. My journey into the valley of contentment has ended. I have arrived in the city of harmony.

13. What need is there for striving or stillness? What is freedom or bondage? What are holy books or teachings? What is the purpose of life? Who is the disciple, and who is the master?

> When there is complete relaxation and a giving up of all striving, then the power of the present is revealed. This power of the moment is overwhelming and humbling. In this moment, the ultimate forces acting in this universe are shown to you.

14. For I have no bounds. I am Shiva. Nothing arises in me, in whom nothing is single, nothing is double. Nothing is. Nothing is not. What more is there to say?

> To exist in the moment is to exist as the highest presence. This highest presence has many names, one of which is Shiva. "I am Shiva!" is the highest expression you are capable of. This expression still takes place in the mind. What you really are is beyond the expressions of the mind. You are the timeless, formless, speechless. You are the pristine Self, forever pure, forever free!

This is the end of Sage Ashtavakra's Song.

Books by the Author:

Living in the Infinite Moment

The Moment of Perfection

The Art of Self-Inquiry

On Clarity And other such Subjects

The Journey Beyond the Word

Journey of the Soul – Into Eternity

Liberation – A Few Words to the Wise

Handbook of Consciousness

There is only One

The Ashtavakra Gita

The Bhagavad Gita

A Writer Writes A Journal

As The Wind Blows

CONTACT INFORMATION

To contact me, send an email to

Jnanichristiankarl@gmail.com

Or

Visit my blog <u>The Art of Self-Inquiry</u>

Thank you for your interest.

Christian Karl

Made in the USA
Monee, IL
24 April 2022

95333160R00069